I0759896

Mastering ITALIAN BREADS

Quarto.com

Originally published as *Tutta l'Italia del pane* by Slow Food Editore © 2024, 2025

Slow Food Editore srl
Via Audisio, 5
12042 Bra (Cn)
tel. 0172 419611
editorinfo@slowfood.it
www.slowfoodeditore.it

English edition first published in 2026 by The Harvard Common Press, an imprint of The Quarto Group,
100 Cummings Center, Suite 265-D, Beverly, MA 01915, USA.
T (978) 282-9590 F (978) 283-2742

EEA Representation, WTS Tax d.o.o.,
Žanova ulica 3, 4000 Kranj, Slovenia.
www.wts-tax.si

The Harvard Common Press titles are also available at discount for retail, wholesale, promotional, and bulk purchase. For details, contact the Special Sales Manager by email at specialsales@quarto.com or by mail at The Quarto Group, Attn: Special Sales Manager, 100 Cummings Center, Suite 265-D, Beverly, MA 01915, USA.

30 29 28 27 26 1 2 3 4 5

ISBN: 978-1-57715-662-8

Digital edition published in 2026
eISBN: 978-1-57715-663-5

Library of Congress Cataloging-in-Publication Data is available.

Design: Roberto Fidale
Page Layout: John Hall Design Group
Photography: Eunice Brovida
Illustration: Silvia Gariglio

The photos and illustrations on pages 37, 39, 40, 42–43, 46–47, 60–61, 66, 74–75, 107 are from Shutterstock.com

ACKNOWLEDGMENTS
Stone Italiana for the White Teti and Grey Argo backgrounds on pages 87, 88, 89, 91, 93, 94, 95, 97, 98, 99, 101, 131, 149, 159, 195, 197, 199, 203, 207, 211, 213, 217, 219, 223, 225, 229, 231
Claudia Deltetto (@clodiaceramics) for the ceramics pages 115, 121, 165, 189, 191, 195, 211, 219, 225

Printed in Guangdong, China TT122025

Mastering ITALIAN BREADS

Recipes *and* Techniques *from* Italy's Most Celebrated Breadmaker

FULVIO MARINO

Author of Italy's Bestselling Bread Books

The past mixed with the present gives birth to the future. The same is true when it comes to baking: We cannot look forward without first embracing our roots.

CONTENTS

INTRODUCTION

A CELEBRATION OF ARTISAN BREADMAKING

I would like to tell you a story.
A beautiful story.
About a loaf of bread.
What do you see when you look at a loaf of bread?

I see a story rich in people and the places they have lived. Some of the best bread has taken thousands of years to perfect. Many recipes have evolved and been perfected over thousands of years. Some bread starters are thousands of years old, too. To me, a perfectly golden, crusty loaf of bread represents years of mistakes, hunger, trials, wars, and happy times.

This is not a book about the history of bread; it is a book about people and places. Above all, it's a celebration of Italian breads and the traditions behind them. By making a traditional bread in our own homes, we keep tradition alive and ensure that it is not forgotten. A bread, a pizza, or a cake in Italy is an expression of a place, and by baking and recreating these classics, I hope to give life to the great Italian tradition of leavened foods and bring the flavors of my region to your kitchen.

Twenty-four years ago, I started making sourdough and realized that from the early 1900s to the present there has been a vacuum. With the advent of brewer's yeast, mother yeast (also known as sourdough starter) was nearly abandoned. Only a few communities continued to use the fermented water and flour mixture in the traditional way.

I still remember the first time I asked my grandfather Felice, born in 1923, if he knew what that mother yeast was. He replied confidently, "Sure, it's that piece of bread dough that comes off at the end of the dough and is stored in the cupboard for the next loaf." A loaf of bread that might have been made a week or even two weeks later, when that dough was "revived" with more flour and more water and, once it had risen, was added to the bread dough. Since the 1900s, we've been using carry-over dough instead. Authentic mother yeast is not created on the spot; it takes at least a month of constant, daily work. In short, it is a product that is not easy to manage and was hard to find in the early 1900s. By bringing it back into existence, we reawaken traditions that would otherwise be lost, revive forgotten breads, and, consequently, rediscover stories of people and places that make our gastronomic knowledge authentic and biodiverse. This is true of all traditional Italian recipes: If we do not commit ourselves to studying and replicating them, we will lose an entire national heritage.

This book aims to do its part and teach you how to bake at home the great bread, pizza, and dessert classics that the whole world envies.

A loaf of bread is a world in itself.

Inside a loaf of bread are not only its ingredients, but also knowledge, joys, sorrows, people, and places…

These breads and leavened goods demarcate regional boundaries and tell the story of the places where they are born and grow, across the Italian peninsula from North to South. Think of rye from the Alps or spelt from the Apennines, regional chestnut breads and so on. They also tell of historical periods and needs. One example is the small loaves that arose in the cities of Northern Italy where consumerism was beginning to take hold: For bakers, bread, which was no longer made at home, was best bought every day, and small sandwiches were perfect for a quick snack at lunchtime. In the South, on the other hand, bread was baked in the countryside once every ten or fifteen days, and large loaves stored well between each baking.

In the mountains, to top it off, whole wheat flour was used and breads were baked as rarely as a couple of times a year, then stored dry for long periods. From a need and/or "scarcity" came true regional specialties like *Ur-paarl* in Trentino-Alto Adige, a rye known for its ability to keep for long periods of time.

But back to the story I want to tell you: a story that will make you never see a loaf of bread the way you used to. It is a story that makes us think about the importance and respect that we owe to bread—which, alas, all too often we do not give.

Let us take a single loaf of bread. Let's say it's a little over 2 pounds (1 kg). To understand its richness, let's look at how many individual grains it takes to make that loaf. Would you have guessed 20,000 grains of wheat? That is 800 heads of grain that would need about 20 to 40 square feet of land to grow.

A 1 KILOGRAM (2.2-POUND) LOAF OF BREAD

↓

FROM 20 TO 40 SQUARE FOOT PLOT OF LAND

Have you ever thought about it?

Those grains that have been sown according to the climate and the land available to the farmers who took care of them will give rise, year by year, to results that are always different and always unique. Once harvested, depending on the miller who selected them, cleaned them, and finally milled them, they will become different flours, which are also unique. But it doesn't end there. The recipe used, the type of yeast chosen, the amount of water added, the type of fermentation, and last but not least, the hands that worked that dough, the shape given, the degree of baking, and the oven are all variables that will contribute to a unique and unrepeatable result. Always keep that in mind. Even though you are starting with the same ingredients, each loaf will be different from the next, one of a kind, just like us.

Places, people, square feet, and recipes.

Well, now that you know this, every time you make a loaf of bread at home or buy it from a bakery, remember that you have a responsibility to celebrate a place and to respect and value the loaf you bake or buy (and therefore not waste a single crumb).

You've probably figured it out. This book is not just a recipe book. It is a book that aims to put bread at its very heart and reveal its story, whether you choose to buy it from a skilled artisan or whether, like so many now, you want to put it to the test by kneading and baking it in your own kitchen at home. In Italy we have one of the largest varieties of wheats, common and durum, and, consequently, of bread products. We are a nation that boasts an exceptional biodiversity, like few others in in the world: Every region, every province, every city, every town, and every hamlet has its own typical product, and by recounting a few of them, these pages aim to celebrate them all.

It is estimated that there are more than 200 types of breads with distinct characteristics on our peninsula. If we include regional varieties, that number increases to over 1,500. If you visit, in whichever region or regions you visit, you'll find a special bread. Whichever town or village you stop in will have their own unique bread.

These many varieties of breads are a symbol of our civilization. They are so important because they tell a story about us. They are the result of our ability and skill in transforming ingredients; in fact, they were created when humans began to think about foods in a complex way through a processes of transformation.

Bread is the result of our intelligence and our ability to understand nature and interact with it to create amazing things.

Bread needs people. It is not produced by nature, but without nature it cannot exist. It is a result of human intelligence and a result of our intellectual evolution. Bread is an intellectual product and a product of our social evolution.

NOTE ABOUT INGREDIENT MEASUREMENTS IN THIS BOOK

Professional bakers measure ingredients by *weight* almost always using grams (not pounds), instead of relying on *volume* measurements. This is true both for dry ingredients, such as flour or sugar, and for liquid ingredients, such as water or lemon juice. Increasingly, home bakers are adopting this valuable habit, because they find it yields better results. That is because weight is more precise than volume. Volume measurements vary by how densely the ingredient is packed in the measuring vessel and also by how the cook looks at ("eyeballs") the volume measurement to see what it shows. **For these reasons, this book uses weight measurements in grams throughout.** You will need a kitchen scale that shows grams; these scales are widely available in all countries, even ones not on the metric system, and they are not expensive. If you do not already have a kitchen scale, I encourage you to get one. You will be pleased with the improvement in the breads and other baked things you are making. Once you get used to it, you will even find, as I do, that measuring by weight goes faster than measuring by volume—another valuable benefit.

A NOTE ABOUT PROOFING TEMPERATURES

Professional bread bakeries typically proof doughs at a temperature significantly above room temperature, usually around 95°F (35°C). If you own a countertop proofer, this is ideal. If you don't, then look for a warm place in your house such as above the refrigerator (heat rises), near a preheated oven, or simply a sunny spot. If there isn't a warm place in your house, allow more time for the dough to rise.

CHAPTER 1

WHEATS AND OTHER BREAD GRAINS OF ITALY

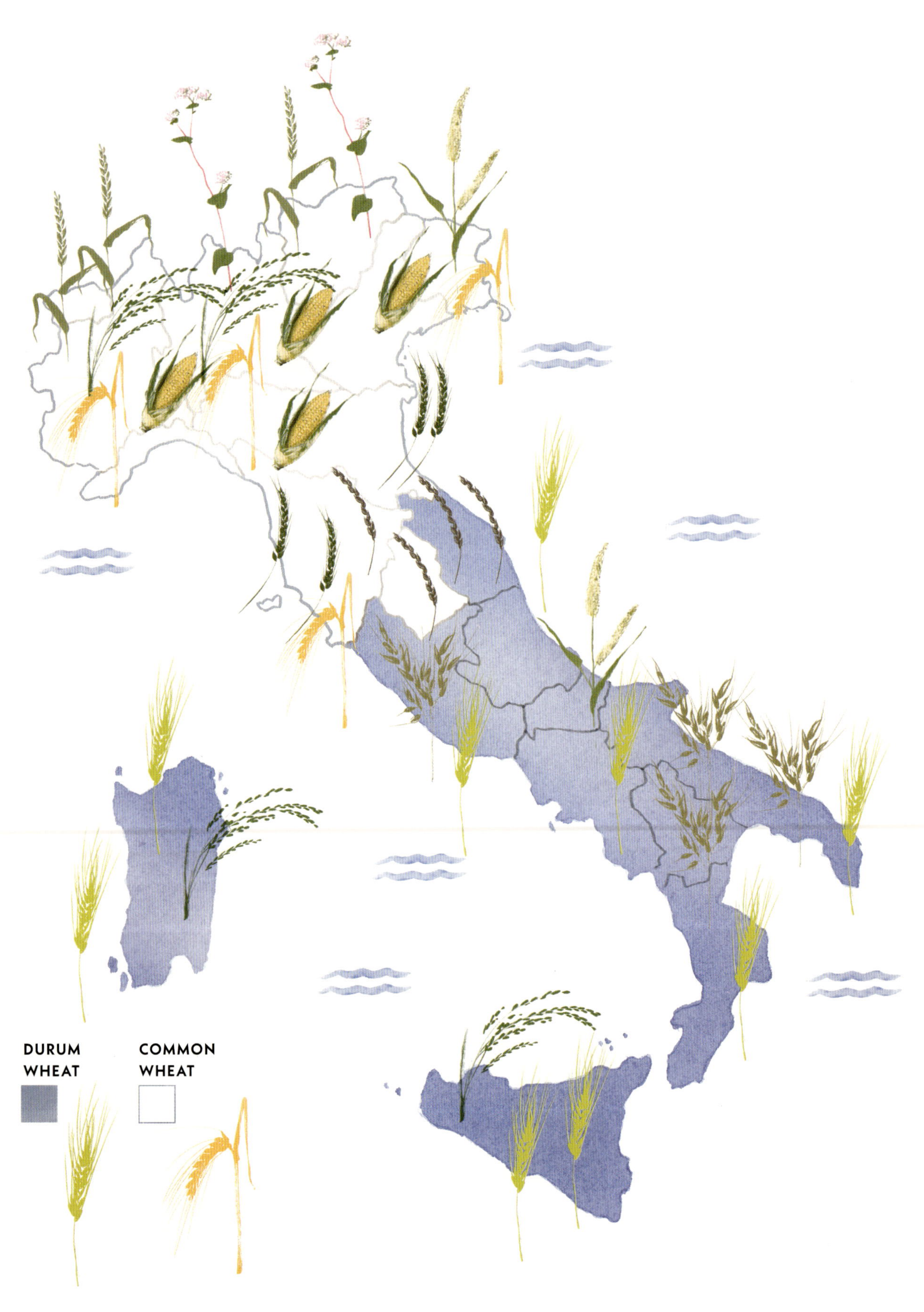
DURUM
WHEAT
COMMON
WHEAT

GRAINS OF ITALY

Common Wheat

This is the type of grain we are all familiar with. In Italy, it is widespread mainly in the North, especially in the Po Valley.

Durum Wheat

Widespread in Central Italy, the South, and the islands. There is a large concentration in Puglia and the central part of Sicily.

Farro

Widespread in Central Italy in the hilly areas of Tuscany, Umbria, and Marche, farro refers to three ancient varieties of wheat. While small (*Triticum monococcum*, or einkorn) and medium (*Triticum dicoccum*, or emmer) varieties are evenly spread, the largest (*Triticum spelta*, or spelt) is found mainly in the South.

Rye

This mountain grain is found mainly in Aosta Valley and Alto Adige.

Rice

Cultivated mainly in Lombardy and Piedmont (93 percent of national production), it is also found in Sicily and Sardinia.

Corn

Particularly widespread in the Po Valley. After its introduction in Europe, it effectively replaced millet.

Buckwheat

Grown in the alpine valleys of Northern Italy and in some areas of the Northern Apennines.

Barley

Grown mainly in Tuscany and Emilia-Romagna, it can still be found throughout the peninsula.

Oats

Its cultivation has almost disappeared in the North, but it is still widespread in Puglia, Basilicata, and Lazio.

Millet

After being supplanted for many years by corn, its cultivation has resumed in parts of Northern Italy.

WHEAT

SCIENTIFIC NAME
Triticum aestivum
COMMON NAME
Common wheat

SCIENTIFIC NAME
Triticum durum
COMMON NAME
Durum wheat

Appearance

THE HEAD

Durum wheat is known for having a head with long bristles, known as awns. Meanwhile, common wheat grows both with and without these bristles.

THE KERNELS

Common wheat is a soft, tender grain. The Italian name for this grain is *grano tenero*, which translates to "tender" or "soft" wheat. From its milling, you get white flour. Durum wheat, on the other hand, is a very stout and glassy grain, and is used in semolina, a flour known for its coarse texture.

Varieties

COMMON WHEAT

Today, many common wheat varieties sown in Italy are the result of selection to find the best ones according to their intended use (bread, cookies, etc.). Many are commercial varieties, some protected by patent. We mention only a few of the longest-lived: *algeri, altamira, bianca lancia, Bologna, bramante, costante, dalì, drusilla, giorgione, lancillotto, ligabue, Monviso, perugino, verna.*

LOCAL ECOTYPES PROTECTED BY SLOW FOOD'S ARK OF TASTE

Bianco delle valli di Suvero (Liguria region), *solina* (Abruzzo Apennines region), *casorella* (Abruzzo region), *carosella* (Basilicata, Campania regions)

DURUM WHEAT

Among the Italian varieties, there has been a great rediscovery of ancient varieties in recent years, in spite of the availability of more commercial ones. The following list indicates the ancient ones with an A in parentheses: *ciccio, colosseo, duilio, Gargano, gentil rosso* (A), *iride, jervicella* (A), *Ofanto, orobel, perciasacchi* (A), *Rieti originario* (A), *senatore Cappelli* (A), *simeto, svevo.*

LOCAL ECOTYPES PROTECTED BY SLOW FOOD'S ARK OF TASTE

Marzellina, saragolla, (Campania region), *timilia* (Sicily)

In the Kitchen

COMMON WHEAT

It is mainly used for bread, pizza, focaccia, desserts (including the great sweet breads: *panettone, pandoro, colomba*), *piadina romagnola, crescia, tigella*, and fresh egg pasta, and it is the main grain for the Neapolitan *pastiera.*

DURUM WHEAT

In southern regions, it replaces common wheat flour in breads, flatbreads, and even in some cakes. These include Matera or Altamura bread, but also Palermo's *sfincione*. In some traditional recipes, it is mixed with common wheat flour, for example in Bari focaccia. It is, moreover, the main ingredient in dry pasta.

Flavor

Common wheat is more neutral than durum wheat, which has a slightly stronger flavor. Much depends on the type of milling and sieving of the flour: The more whole grain the flour contains, the more flavorful it will be. Of course, variety also matters as some, with the same flour processing, give a richer flavor.

Flours

COMMON WHEAT

00, 0, 1, 2, whole wheat, cracked wheat, common wheat bran, common wheat kernels

DURUM WHEAT

Semola, semolina, whole grain semolina, remilled couscous, bulgur

Historic Background

During the 16th century, wheat was introduced by the Spaniards to North America. Due to the interruption of American imports from Russia, it became the largest exporter as a result of the strong impetus given to the cultivation and selection of varieties according to the industrial needs during World War I.

Nutritional Information

The outermost surface of the grain is the bran, or cortical part, which is rich in fiber and protein. Inside the grains is the endosperm, or albumen, which makes up 83 percent of the caryopsis. Wheat consists mostly of carbohydrates but also provides a good amount of protein. It has high satiating power and contains no cholesterol.

Did you know...

The DNA complex of wheat is five times larger than the human genome and consists of 17 billion "letters." Scientists from the University of Liverpool, Bristol, and the John Innes Centre (an independent international research center in Britain) discovered this.

FARRO

SCIENTIFIC NAME
Triticum monococcum
COMMON NAME
Einkorn or *farro piccolo*

SCIENTIFIC NAME
Triticum dicoccum
COMMON NAME
Emmer or *farro medio*

SCIENTIFIC NAME
Triticum spelta
COMMON NAME
Spelt or *farro grande*

Appearance

THE HEAD

That of *T. Monococcum* or einkorn is smaller than the other varieties and composed of a single row of grains. In contrast, *T. dicoccum* or emmer has a larger head, composed of two rows of grains. The head of *T. spelta* or spelt is more similar to common wheat and darker in color.

THE GRAINS

When farro is harvested and threshed, the grains are still covered by a tough hull and must be husked. Thus, after harvesting, you do not have naked grains that are ready to be milled. Instead, intermediate processing is required to remove the husk.

Varieties

The main varieties of farro are *T. monococcum*, called einkorn or *farro piccolo* (small farro), *T. dicoccum*, called emmer or *farro medio* (medium farro), and *T. spelta*, called spelt or *farro grande* (large farro). Einkorn is the oldest variety of farro that is available today.

LOCAL ECOTYPES PROTECTED BY SLOW FOOD'S ARK OF TASTE

Alvese rosso (Parco del Gran Sasso region), *Garfagnana spelt* (Tuscany region)

In the Kitchen

EINKORN

When turned into flour, it makes great tarts, cookies, breads, and buns with short leavening. As a whole grain, it is wonderful in salads and soups.

EMMER

When milled into flour, emmer, the most widely available variety of farro, is best used in egg-based pasta, bread, pizzas, and flatbreads. As a whole grain, it is a hearty addition to soups and salads.

SPELT

As a flour, spelt is perfect for cookies, crackers, and eggless dry pasta. In its whole form, it can be used in soups and salads, just like emmer and einkorn.

Flavor

In general, farro has a decidedly more pronounced and "rounded" flavor than common wheat and durum wheat. It is delicate but suitable for all kinds of dishes because it does not overpower the other flavors. Some subtle differences can be detected between the varieties: Einkorn is more intense and tastes almost almondy, emmer is slightly more herbaceous or leathery, and spelt is the most delicate.

Flours

EINKORN

White, whole grain

EMMER

Semolina, whole grain semolina

SPELT

White, whole grain

Historic Background

Researchers have found evidence of wild wheat as early as 23,000 years ago (near Lake Tiberias in Israel). It was around 10,000 to 12,000 years ago that society switched from a nomadic lifestyle to an agrarian one and that's when we first see *Triticum monococcum*, the ancestor of modern cereals. Later spontaneous cross-fertilization led to *Triticum dicoccum*, an ancestor of durum wheat, and then spelt, the ancestor of common wheat.

Nutritional Information

Farro is rich in protein and antioxidants (like polyphenols and selenium), contains less gluten than wheat, and has a low glycemic index.

Did you know...

The word *farro* comes from the Latin *far*, the same root as the Italian word for flour, *farina*. Despite being among the oldest grains, it is now often considered a gourmet ingredient in Italian cuisine.

RYE

SCIENTIFIC NAME
Secale cereale
COMMON NAME
Rye

Appearance

THE HEAD

Rye has a head with very thin whiskers that are narrower and longer than that of wheat.

THE GRAINS

The grains of rye have a distinctive greenish color, unlike most other grains.

Varieties

Segale invernale or *grande segale*, *segale estiva* or *segale dormiente* (winter rye, fall rye, and summer rye)

In the Kitchen

In cooking, we find rye in traditional soups, such as Valtellina *süpa sciücia* (a popular soup in Italy that translates to "rye bread soup"). Its flour is used to make breads and baked goods, some of which can keep for almost a year if stored properly. Outside of sourdough, it's the only grain known for making baked goods that last so long.

Flavor

The taste is unique, almost herbaceous, and lingers on the palate for a long time. It is a favorite of true bread connoisseurs. Rye can be tricky to work with, so I have included lots of tips on how to use it (see pages 72 and 73).

Flours

In the United States, you will find it labeled "medium rye flour" and "dark rye flour." In Europe, it is milled into 00, 0, 1, 2, and whole grain.

Historic Background

Rye originated in Asia Minor, beginning to grow among farro and wheat, and was first seen as a weed. In colder areas, rye thrives and tends to overpower wheat. Some might say that makes it an appealing plant for human sustenance. In Italy, it is a staple crop of northern populations.

Nutritional Information

Rye contains a low amount of gluten and a lot of fiber. Because of this, it is known to help keep blood sugar and cholesterol levels under control. It is high in antioxidants, and some studies show that it can reduce inflammation.

Did you know...

In recent years, the largest producer of rye in Italy has been in the southwest region of Calabria, where it grows mainly in national parks. In the United States, it is grown mainly in the Midwest in states like Minnesota and Wisconsin.

RICE

SCIENTIFIC NAME
Oryza sativa
COMMON NAME
Rice

Appearance

THE HEAD

During the summer, the rice plant produces a flower cluster, the panicle, often incorrectly called a head. The panicle contains many spikelets, each with flowers.

THE GRAINS

As with corn, it is difficult to give an unequivocal description of the many varieties. A glassy appearance is common in almost all varieties, while colors vary from white to red to black.

Varieties

In Italy, rice is typically divided into four groups:

COMMON small and round grains

SEMI-FINE medium-length round grains

FINE tapered grains

SUPER FINE long grains

In the United States, you will mainly find short-grain rice (such as sushi rice), medium-grain rice (like Calrose), and long-grain rice.

LOCAL ECOTYPES PROTECTED BY SLOW FOOD'S ARK OF TASTE

Gigante Vercelli, Maratelli, razza 77 (Piedmont region), *di Grumolo delle Abbadesse* (Veneto region)

In the Kitchen

Rice works well in a variety of dishes, from risottos to pilafs and puddings. To give just a few examples, think of fried rice, paella, red beans and rice, or stuffed peppers. It's a great base for both savory and sweet dishes (rice pudding or horchata, anyone?). When it comes to baking, it is found in gluten-free desserts like cakes.

Flavor

It is difficult to identify a single definite flavor in the face of such great biodiversity. However, a good rice should have moderate sweetness and acidity and subtle bitterness.

Flours

In the United States, rice is typically milled into white rice flour, brown rice flour, or glutinous rice flour (also known as sweet white rice flour). In Italy, it can be milled into white flour, whole grain flour, rice meal, whole grain, or rice semolina.

Historic Background

It is unclear where rice originated. Some speculate that the first varieties emerged more than 12,000 years ago in the foothills of the Himalayas somewhere between Nepal and India. Some archaeological finds show the presence of cultivated rice and wild varieties in China as early as the 6th millennium BCE.

Nutritional Information

Rice is rich in starch—its caryopsis can contain up to 80 percent of it. While it is lower in protein compared to other cereals, it is energy-rich and highly digestible.

Did you know...

Rice is certainly one of the most iconic ingredients in the world. Italy produces more than 50 percent of the rice grown throughout Europe.

CORN

SCIENTIFIC NAME
Zea mays
COMMON NAME
Corn or maize

Appearance

THE EAR

When it comes to appearance, corn noticeably differs from other grains. The male flowers of the corn plant have long tassels whereas the female corn plants grow ears with silks.

THE GRAINS

Corn kernels are diverse and come in many colors, from white to yellow. You'll even find it in blue, black, and purple.

Italian Varieties

PEARL WHITE FLINTS

Biancoperla, righetta bianco, cimalunga

LATE SOUTHERN CYLINDRICAL FLINTS

Montoro, rodindia, pannaro

MIDSEASON SOUTHERN CYLINDRICAL FLINTS

Trentinella, dindico, altosiculo

CONICAL FLINTS AND DERIVATIVES

Barbina, poliranghi, montano, biancone, ostesa

DENT CORN

Dentati bianchi antichi, dentati moderni

MICROSPERMA FLINTS

Zeppetello, cinquantino Marano, quarantino estivo, Cadore

EXTRA-EARLY DWARF FLINTS

Poliota, trenodi, tirolese

EIGHT-ROWED FLINTS AND DERIVATIVES

Ottofile puri, razze derivate

PADANIANS

Rostrato-scagliolo, bani-scaiola, agostano

LOCAL ECOTYPES PROTECTED BY SLOW FOOD'S ARK OF TASTE

Agostinella (Lazio region), *biancoperla* (Presidio, Veneto regions), *cinquantino bianco di Gemona, cinquantino giallo di Claut, cinquantino rosso di Buja, dente di cavallo, pignoletto della Val Cosa, resiano, rosso di Aquileia, rosso di San Martino, socchievina* (Friuli-Venezia Giulia region), *ganassina, Marano, nero spinoso della Valle Camonica, ottofile del Pavese, rostrato rosso di Rovetta, san Pancrazio, scagliolo di Carenno, spinato di Gandino* (Lombardy region), *ostenga del Canavese, ottofile, pignoletto rosso del Canavese* (Piedmont region), *ottofile di Roccacontrada* (Marche region), *spin della Valsugana* (Trentino-Alto Adige region), *sponcio* (Veneto region), *trentolino* (Tuscany region), *quarantino* (Abruzzo, Lombardy, Marche, Tuscany regions)

In the Kitchen

Corn yields a starch that works well as a thickener in things like custards and pies. It can be used in cookies, breads, and muffins. Corn that is used in leavened products should be precooked and boiled (gelatinized) to make it more workable.

Flavor

Corn is traditionally known for its sweetness, which can be more or less pronounced depending on the variety.

Flours

In Italy: *Bramata* (coarse-grained), *fioretto* (medium-fine-grained), *fumetto* (fine-grained, similar to common wheat flour)

In the US: finely ground corn flour, stone-ground corn flour, cornmeal, masa harina

Did you know...

On average, an ear of corn contains around 800 kernels?

Historic Background

Much as grains mark the beginning of the birth of Mediterranean agriculture in the Fertile Crescent, corn initiated the agricultural process about 9,000 years ago among the peoples of Mexico and South America. It spread to the United States and Canada, and arrived in Europe after 1492. In Italy, corn abruptly replaced millet, which until then was one of the most widely cultivated plants, and became the staple food of many Italian peasants.

Nutritional Information

A naturally gluten-free grain, corn is known for being low-fat, high-fiber, and full of antioxidants.

BUCKWHEAT

SCIENTIFIC NAME
Fagopyrum esculentum
COMMON NAME
Buckwheat

Appearance

THE PLANT

Buckwheat is an annual plant with a reddish branched hollow stem that grows about 32 to 48 inches (81 to 122 cm) tall. Its sharp, heart- or arrow-shaped leaves have the peculiarity of being sessile (attached directly to the stem) at the top and petiolate toward the bottom. The flowers are small, numerous, and arranged in short, close clusters at the ends of the sprigs.

THE GRAINS

Buckwheat's grains are gray and slightly convex. In contrast, the grains of Japanese buckwheat are browner, larger, and distinctly triangular in shape. The grain's resemblance to the fruit of the beech tree (*fagum* in Latin) is the source of the plant's scientific name.

Varieties

In Italy: common buckwheat, La Harpe (developed by the Institut national de la recherche agronomique in France), Japanese buckwheat

In the US: The United States grows both common buckwheat (*Fagopyrum esculentum*) and Tartary buckwheat (*Fagopyrum tartaricum*), but you'll mostly find the grain simply labeled "buckwheat."

LOCAL ECOTYPES PROTECTED BY SLOW FOOD'S ARK OF TASTE

Valnerina (Umbria region), *Valtellina* (Lombardy region), *di Terragnolo* (Trentino region)

In the Kitchen

As a grain, it is ideal for enriching soups or salads. Thanks to its flavor, it is used to prepare fresh pastas (in Italy, it is used in a flat ribbon pasta called *pizzoccheri*) and, in combination with other flours, to give a unique flavor to breads and cakes. Taking a leap into French cuisine, we cannot fail to mention its use in Breton galettes. Buckwheat is a key ingredient in the cookie.

Flavor

The taste of buckwheat flour is very distinctive: a full flavor with notes of nuts and malt. It is slightly bitter on the palate, but not unpleasantly so. On the contrary, this note gives a touch of complexity. When cooked, buckwheat flour gives off an intense aroma similar to that of freshly baked bread.

Flours

Whole grain, white

Historic Background

Buckwheat seems to have been cultivated since the 5th and 6th centuries CE, most likely originating in China before making its way to Japan and India. It was not until the Middle Ages that it reached Europe, perhaps introduced by Mongol peoples whose migrations allowed its propagation initially in Poland and Germany. Its cultivation then spread to France and, later, to regions of Austria and Northern Italy.

Nutritional Information

The chemical composition of buckwheat is very similar to that of cereals from grasses in terms of starch (65 to 70 percent), fiber (around 10 percent), and fat (around 2 percent). The protein content ranges from 10 to 13 percent. Its protein is of high biological value, containing significant amounts of essential amino acids, such as lysine and tryptophan, not usually found so much in other cereals. It is rich in folic acid and naturally gluten-free.

Did you know...

Buckwheat is often mistakenly included in the Gramineae family (grasses). However, it belongs to the Polygonaceae family, which includes rhubarb. It is usually grouped together with cereals because the grain from which the flour is obtained is ground in the same way, and the composition of the resulting flour is nutritionally very similar to that of graminaceous plants.

BARLEY

SCIENTIFIC NAME
Hordeum vulgare
COMMON NAME
Barley

Appearance

THE HEAD

Barley has longer whiskers than wheat, and the head can have from two to six rows of grains, depending on the variety. In addition, barley caryopses are usually larger than those of wheat. It ripens earlier and its heads are curved downward, while those of wheat remain straight.

THE GRAINS

The grains of barley are yellowish in color, although some varieties may tend to appear white or even red and black. They range in size from ⅓ to ½ inch (8 mm to 1 cm) in length and are ⅒ inch (3 mm) wide.

Varieties

Distic barley (produces one ear with two rows of grains), polystic barley (produces heads with four to six rows of grains).

In the Kitchen

In Italy, barley finds use in some regional peasant breads, which, by tradition, were prepared by adding flour from this cereal especially when harvests were scarce. Barley is ideal for making soups and stews, in salads, and in *orzotto*, where it is cooked like risotto.

Flavor

Barley has a slightly nutty flavor, reminiscent of brown rice and farro. It can sometimes develop bitter notes.

Flours

Whole grain flour (made by milling hulled barley), white flour (made by sifting the fiber from the white inner part of the grain)

Historic Background

This cereal has been used as a food crop since the 7th century BCE. Its very ancient origins are evidenced by the fact that humans in Mesopotamia, in the early days of agriculture, began to cultivate wild barley varieties alongside *Triticum monococcum* (farro), which were later domesticated. It is thus one of the earliest cereals widely cultivated and consumed in the Mediterranean basin.

Nutritional Information

Barley is very rich in carbohydrates and also contains protein, fiber, fat, minerals, and vitamins. It contains gluten, consisting mainly of albumins that, when binding with prolamins and glutenin, give a lower quality gluten mesh than wheat.

Did you know...

Barley can be pearled, hulled, or husked. During husking, it is stripped only of the outermost hull, which makes it easier to cook and process while leaving its nutritional value intact. When it is pearled, the entire outer part, including the bran, is removed, which makes it less rich in fiber but faster to cook. It also becomes lighter in color during this process. You can also find barley flakes, which are made from husked grains that have been moistened and compressed while hot.

OATS

SCIENTIFIC NAME
Avena sativa
COMMON NAME
Oats

Appearance

THE HEAD

Oat spikelets have few grains, are not as compact as those of wheat, and hang from the top of the plant's stem.

THE GRAINS

More elongated and narrower than those of wheat, they have numerous outer fiber layers, significantly more in number than other cereals: It is estimated that up to 45 percent of the caryopsis consists of outer layers. Because the grains are very adherent to the endosperm, they are difficult to separate during milling.

Varieties

Barbata, brevis, clauda, insularis, longiglumis, maggiore, maggiore, saxatilis, selvatica, strigosa

In the Kitchen

The grains are excellent—after adequate soaking—for soups and stews, while the flakes are mainstays in breakfast cereals, but can also be sprinkled on top of bread before baking. Oat flour, when properly mixed with other flours, can make wonderful baked goods like muffins and cakes. Unlock even more nutrients in this ingredient by combining it with sourdough, as the acidity and presence of phytates makes even more nutrients (like zinc and iron) available.

Flavor

Oats have a fairly neutral flavor such that they can be used in both sweet and savory recipes.

Flours

Whole grain, white

Historic Background

The earliest cultivation of oats appears to date back between 3000 and 4000 BCE in the Chinese countryside. In Greek and Roman times, oats were considered less important than barley and wheat. Given their excellent ability to adapt to colder climates, however, they became widely popular among northern European populations (think: porridge).

Nutritional Information

Oatmeal and its derivatives contain a large amount of plant fiber and substances such as beta-glucans that are useful to our bodies. They appear to decrease blood cholesterol levels and may help with weight loss. Oats also have a fat content of 6 to 8 percent, much higher than that of other cereals, and they therefore have a higher energy value. The grain is rich in vitamins A (beta-carotene), B, D, and E, as well as a natural antioxidant that protects against free radicals.

Did you know...

Oats are a hardy plant that is frequently considered a weed within crops of other cereals.

MILLET

SCIENTIFIC NAME
Panicum miliaceum
COMMON NAME
Millet

Appearance

THE HEAD

The spikes are small in size and generally do not exceed 1½ inches (4 cm). They contain a limited number of flowers and, later, fruits inside of which the seeds are contained.

THE GRAINS

They can be many colors, depending on the variety: from yellow to black to greenish to purple. They have an elliptical shape and shiny appearance and are up to seven times smaller than wheat.

Varieties

White, Japanese, Indian, silky, kodo

In the Kitchen

When used whole, millet can be found in meatballs, flans, and pies, as well as in cakes and puddings. Pastries, crackers, and cookies can be made with the flour. It can be used in gluten-free cooking and baking. It combines well with other flours.

Flavor

It has a sweet and delicate flavor that lends itself to many cooking and baking applications from the most delicate to the most daring.

Flours

Whole grain, white

Historic Background

Millet is an ancient grain native to Africa and Asia. Before the arrival of corn, it was also very common in Europe. It was used in everyday life and was the basic ingredient in polenta. Now it is grown only marginally in Italy, but in Africa it still forms the basis of staple foods. Slow Food has been protecting a Ugandan variety of it and many traditional varieties are protected by its Ark of Taste project.

Nutritional Information

It contains approximately the same amount of protein as other cereals, less starch, and abundant amounts of lipids, so much so that vegetable oil is often produced from the germ. Millet contains no gluten and can therefore be used by people with celiac disease.

Did you know...

Millet is a very resilient cereal that adapts well to even the most difficult climatic areas: Once sown, it does not require much care. Because of this, it may adapt well to climate change. When harvested, it must be husked, and it loses half its weight during that process.

FROM CEREALS TO FLOURS

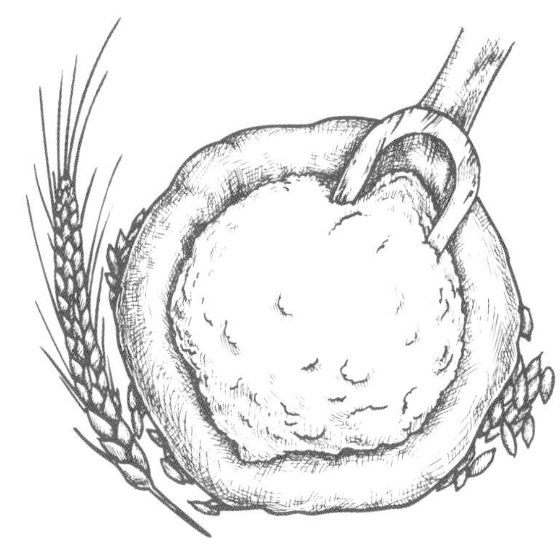

Flour Analysis and the Tools Needed

To be a good baker one must also be a bit of a miller. If you've reviewed the grain profiles on the previous pages, you have a head start. Knowing the wider world of flours allows you to always choose the most suitable one for the recipe you have in mind. This will help you achieve the best result.

The miller's work is decisive: If an exceptional or superior grain is processed without any skill, the result is usually a mediocre bread, pizza, or cake. On the other hand, if the intrinsic characteristics of the starting grain are preserved in the flour, the result is often stunning.

In our family mill, before we buy any shipment of wheat or other cereal, we carry out **sampling** in order to analyze it. We first carry out a **visual and olfactory observation** to see how healthy the grains are and whether there are any impurities. Then, we perform **microbiological and rheological analysis** (rheology is the study of deformation of a matter subjected to mechanical stress). For the former, we use an independent, European-accredited laboratory that can detect the possible presence of any of more than six hundred types of pesticides (insecticides, glyphosate, phosphine, growth regulators, herbicides, fungicides, etc.). We always look for a grain that is good but also healthy for the people who will be eating it. We do the rheological tests, however, in our own laboratory: We calculate the specific weight of the grain, the amount of protein, the moisture level, and the enzyme activity. If the sample passes these tests, we purchase it. Then when the shipment is delivered to us, as soon as it is offloaded, we repeat the analysis process as I described it earlier, to make sure that the shipment conforms to the sample.

For the sake of complete information, let's now schematically review the instruments used for grain analysis to learn more about the technicalities of the valuable work that millers do.

NEAR-INFRARED SPECTROSCOPY (NIR)

This is a spectrophotometer that measures the electromagnetic spectrum of grains with infrared rays. It is used to detect **moisture content** and the **amount of protein**.

CHOPIN ALVEOGRAPH

This measures the **strength**, **tenacity**, and **extensibility** of a dough. Small amounts of flour are mixed with salt water and made into disks, which are inflated with air, and then the expansion is measured by a curved graph. The curves of the various disks are averaged and measured according to the following values: **P**, the maximum height of the curve indicating the **resistance** of the dough; **L**, the length of the curve indicating the **extensibility** of the dough; and **W**, the area of the surface drawn by the curve indicating the **strength** of the flour. This last value is particularly important because it indicates the ability of the flour to absorb liquids during mixing and kneading and its ability to hold gases during rising.

BRABENDER FARINOGRAPH

This measures the force required to create a dough of water and flour. It is basically a small kneading machine connected to a dynamometer. It gives us data on the **absorption of the flour**, the time it takes to get to optimal dough conditions, the time the dough will remain stable, and when it will begin to deteriorate.

FALLING NUMBER

This measures the activity of enzymes in the flour. It helps us understand whether we are dealing with flours that may be too sticky once kneaded, or whether they need intermediate sugars, such as malt, in order to be baked optimally.

HERE ARE THE POSSIBLE CLASSIFICATIONS AFTER THESE ANALYSES. THESE ARE APPROXIMATE BUT USEFUL TO THE MILLER IN CHOOSING A PARTICULAR FLOUR OR MAKING BLENDS.

P/L	
> 1	the flour is very tenacious and resistant
< 0.5	the flour is very extensible
W	
> 400	the flour is very strong
330/350	the flour is strong
280/300	the flour is normal strength
200/250	the flour is medium strength
< 200	the flour is weak

Cleaning the Grains

An essential step that rests with the miller, after choosing the best raw materials, is to do some "cleaning." I want to let you in on a secret. Despite the fact that few people talk about it, if you want quality, grain cleaning is crucial. Any mill that offers high-quality flours should have a modern facility for cleaning the raw material. The grain that comes from the fields is always full of impurities: sand, soil, stones and pebbles, fragments of other seeds, even bits of metal or moldy grains. It is essential that the grain be stored in a dry and clean place so that it will keep for long periods.

We have **twelve cleaning steps** at our mill. **Pre-cleaning** removes the "coarser" impurities. Next, we **de-stone**. As the word suggests, this is when we remove stones and pebbles, from the grain. Then, we use a **wet cleaning** process, which washes and scrubs the raw material to remove as much dust as possible. Next, we use various **brushes and screens** to remove other impurities. Finally, we use an **optical sorter**. This device uses NASA-developed technology to check each individual grain and separate out those with defects in shape or color. But that's not all: Using infrared rays, it also checks the caryopses, which isolates harmful fungi or bacteria. After this, the grain is **"conditioned,"** that is, tempered in different ways depending on the type. For this step, the miller's skill should be reminiscent of that of the baker. Depending on the hardness, they will need to add more or less water and let the grains **rest** from six to forty-eight hours before grinding. This will make the caryopses more tender and elastic.

The Industrial Revolution and Flour

The cylinder mill was one of the first tools to revolutionize industrial food production, laying the foundation for everything it would later become and still is today. The British manufacturing revolution of the late 19th century was also about food, not just manufactured goods and engineering works. The first plants to produce flour were established. It was then that the many stone mills, found in every neighborhood or town, were replaced by a few large cylinder mills: They guaranteed whiter flours that were easier to store because the germ was removed. The germ is the most important part of the grain nutritionally but also the most difficult to store. White bread, in those days, was seen as something for the rich, and making "clean" flours accessible to all was a social achievement for many. Extremely white flours have, however, deprived us of an essential component. Even the manufacturers have realized this, and, if we look at the white flours sold in American or British supermarkets, by law they are fortified with folic acid, riboflavin, and more. Regulations seek to restore what milling has taken away just as synthetic flavorings are added to many other overprocessed foods to restore aroma and taste. But why add what was removed before after the fact?

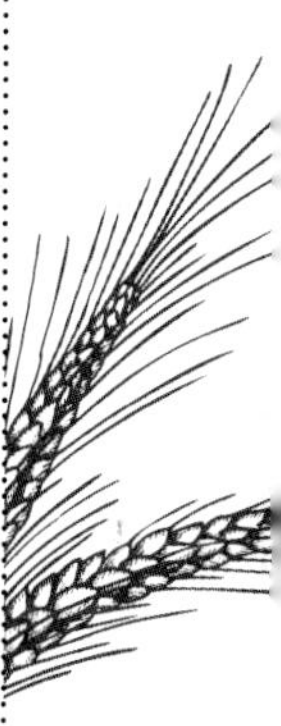

Milling

CYLINDER MILLING

In cylinder milling, grains are processed with large cast-iron and steel rollers. These rollers, or rolling mills, are divided into three types: breaking mills, stripping mills, and regrinding mills.

Breaking rollers are used to strip off the outermost parts of the grain, while **stripping rollers** scrape off the flour fragments present in the bran residue. Finally, the **regrinding rollers** turn the whiter, bran-free parts into flour.

Between each step, the grains are put through large sieves, called **plansifters**. These manage to divide and sort the matter coming off the rolls for subsequent steps. The more granular or "semolina-like" parts are sent to other special machinery called **purifiers**. The flour obtained at the end of these stages is very white. The grain, in fact, is **"degerminated,"** that is, stripped of the germ, which is the fattest part of the caryopsis.

With cylinder milling, therefore, the germ is lost, and, if for whatever reason you decide you still want to have it in the flour, roasting and stabilization processes are required to incorporate it at the end. The same goes for the other "whole" parts of the grain, which include the outermost fibers of the caryopsis and the so-called "aleurone layer," the intermediate part between the white interior of the grain and the outer bran. Producing a whole grain flour with cylinders is rather cumbersome, because all the removed parts have to be brought together afterward in order to "reconstruct" the flour.

STONE MILLING (NATURAL OR MODERN)

In stone milling, the grains are processed in a single stage through **two circular stones placed one on top of the other**. The resulting flour is a complete whole grain flour. Inside it are all the parts of the grain and, if you want to make it whiter, it is processed through a special sieve called a **tumbler**. The degree of sifting determines whether a flour is classified as semi-whole meal, type 1, or type 2 (a classification used in Italy, for more on this see page 44).

But how do the two stones work? One is stationary while the other rotates by levering a central pole that keeps it balanced. The grains are fed into the center and then pass through channels leading outward. Due to centrifugal force, they come out as flour. The two stones never touch each other—they have no friction whatsoever. It is the flour that acts as a bearing: It turns one stone on top of the other. The stones are usually ⅒ inch (3 mm) apart. Of course, there is always a need for some balancing to achieve the right grading of flour. This is why the artisanal work of the miller is based on experience handed down from one generation to the next. There are no schools that teach this, and it is not enough to have a good stone mill to have quality flours: A miller's individual expertise is required.

It should be added that two types of stones are available for stone grinding today: **natural** ones and **modern** ones.

Natural stones can be of various origins. Those in my family, for example, are made of **molar flint**, a variety of quartz famous for its hardness. In particular, they come from a quarry—now decommissioned—about 60 miles (97 km) from Paris. They are the most sought-after ones to this day because they are perfect for sustaining **hammering**. This, also called **millstone dressing**, is basically the preparation and maintenance of the natural stones in a mill. It has to be done periodically by the miller who takes care of it, using special hammers.

Here is where the human factor emerges again: The grinding is basically the signature that the miller puts on their flour, creating little grooves that help husk the grain and make the milling process as perfect and delicate as possible.

Depending how much you sift and how you sift, you can get semi-whole or type 1 or type 2 flours.

Each grain has its own structure. If you standardize grinding and use the same stone to grind different grains, you will not get the best characteristics of each. At our mill, for example, we have as many as ten different stones. A well-done top grinding, then, makes it possible to not overheat the grains too much and to better preserve the germ so that it does not go rancid during storage. Thanks to the low grinding speed with the natural stone, it is possible to grind grains by providing a lower moisture content than with cylinders, another determining factor for quality. In **modern stone grinding**, on the other hand, millstones are agglomerates made from a **mixture of different materials**, for example, **emery** and **flint**. They are stones invented in the last century and were initially used for grinding grain for animal feed. They also helped replace natural stones. Modern millstones rotate much faster than natural ones, managing to reach 500 or 600 revolutions per minute (as opposed to 100 to 150 revolutions for natural ones), and thus guarantee higher production for the same amount of time. But speed, as we have seen, is a factor that must be controlled and, if possible, avoided in order to have an absolute quality product.

HOW FLOUR IS MADE

1. SAMPLING
A small quantity of grain is taken for analysis by potential buyers.

2. LOOKING AND SMELLING
Buyers check for impurities and imperfections.

3. MICROBIOLOGICAL AND RHEOLOGICAL ANALYSIS
Samples are sent to a lab for further analysis (rheology is the study of deformation of matter subjected to mechanical stress).

4. DELIVERY OF THE GOODS
If the grain has passed all the tests, it is purchased.

5. REPETITION OF 1, 2, AND 3 FOR COMPLIANCE CHECK

The entire batch purchased must conform to the sample.

6. ANALYSIS TOOLS

NIR
Chopin Alveograph
Brabender Farinograph
Falling Number

7. CLEANING

Grain coming from the fields may have a number of impurities such as sand, pebbles, bits of metal, moldy grains, or seeds, so it is cleaned, typically in a twelve-step process.

8. CONDITIONING

The grain is moistened differently depending on the type, hardness, and sensitivity of the miller.

9. REST

Before milling, the grains must rest for six to forty-eight hours.

10. MILLING

CYLINDER

STONE
(natural or modern)

Typologies and Use

Laboratories always do ash analysis before selling flour.

The **amount of ash** actually indicates the amount of fiber present. Some people think this is used to classify flours for a **particular use.** Although we roughly indicate in the table what the final products will be, it is not always the case, for example, that a type 0 flour is ideal for cookies or that a type 00 flour is perfect for leavened products.

When it comes to Italian flour, it is important to assess the **strength of the flour**, because there can be a stronger type 0 and a weaker type 00. This characteristic depends on the grains used, while the type basically indicates whiteness: The more zeros there are, the whiter the flour will be. This division is made based on the **minimum extraction rate**, or sifting rate, which is the amount of flour that is obtained by milling 100 kilograms of grain. The higher the extraction rate, the whiter the flour will be. You can, however, find equivalents in the United States. See the box below.

FLOUR EQUIVALENTS IN THE UNITED STATES

Unlike in Italy, where flours are initially classified by ash content, in the United States, flours are primarily categorized by how much protein they have. While it may be possible to find Italian flours online or in specialty shops, you can use the list below to see which flour may be the most similar to the Italian flours used in the recipes.

Italian 00 flour (8–9% protein, W 0–180) = pastry flour or cake flour

Italian 0 flour (10–12% protein, W 180–240) = all-purpose flour

Italian 1 flour (10–12% protein, W 180–240) = white semi-whole wheat or high-gluten flour

Italian 2 flour (10–13% protein, W 180–350) = white whole wheat or first clear flour

MAXIMUM AMOUNT OF ASH IN ITALIAN FLOURS

TYPE	MINIMUM EXTRACTION RATE	USE	MAXIMUM ASH
00	70%	Neapolitan pizza	0.55%
0	73%	Desserts	0.65%
1	80%	White bread	0.80%
2	90%	Semi-whole grain bread	0.90%
Whole wheat	95%	Whole grain bread	Minimum 1.30%, Maximum 1.70%

ITALIAN FLOUR STRENGTHS AND THEIR USE IN BAKING

TYPE	W 90–170	W 180–250	W 260–350	W >350
00	Cookies, butter-based doughs (such as brisée), sugared dough	Cakes, pastry dough (such as that used for cream puffs), confectionary cream, ordinary short-rising bread	Short-rise pizzas, baguettes, small breads, breads used to make toast	Brioche, thick breads (like babas), long-rise pizzas and doughs
0	Cookies, butter-based dough, sugared dough	Cakes, pastry dough (such as that used for cream puffs), confectionary cream, ordinary short-rise bread	Pastry dough (such as that used for cream puffs), puff pastry, ciabatta, small breads, medium-rise baguettes	Brioche, thick breads, long-rise pizzas and doughs (e.g., panettone), rosettes, ciabatta
1		Plain breads		
2		Plain breads		
Whole wheat		Whole grain breads and pizzas		

Durum Wheat Semolina

The classification regarding durum wheat flours follows a different logic than that for common wheat. The grain of this cereal is vitreous, so grinding it produces a semolina, rather than an actual flour. Durum wheat has a much more tenacious and less elastic gluten, and its average protein value is higher, as is its absorption. In breadmaking, the yield will be completely different.

Semolina is defined by Italian law as follows: "The sharp-edged granular product obtained from the milling and subsequent sifting of durum wheat, freed of foreign matter and impurities."

From the milling of durum wheat, as we have seen in the cereal fact sheet, it is possible to produce semolina, whole wheat semolina, and remilled semolina.

HOW TO CHOOSE A FLOUR

In order to best pick a flour, you need to know the types of grains and the strengths of each type of flour, but there are also other approaches that I would recommend when selecting a flour.

CHECK THE TYPE OF CEREAL

from which the flour you want to buy is made, such as whether it is composed of only one grain or a mix (in this case, the various flours will be listed on the label in descending order and, in the case of different cereals, the percentage will be shown).

CHECK THE DEGREE OF SIFTING

that is, the type of flour (00, 0, 1, 2, or whole grain in Italy) to see whether it contains all the grain components or not.

CHECK WHERE IT WAS PRODUCED AND BY WHOM

Sometimes if you don't have direct information, you can search online to find out where the flour was milled and, in general, what the miller's production philosophy is.

CHECK WHETHER THE FLOUR IS CERTIFIED ORGANIC

In Italy, it will have a green mark with a leaf along with the code of the authorized inspection body and the number of the operator who carried out the verification. In the United States, look for the USDA Organic label. In the United Kingdom, look for a BDA Certification: Organic label.

CHECK THE STRENGTH OF THE FLOUR

If it is not specifically stated on the label, you can figure it out according to the amount of protein found in the nutrition panel.

CHECK THE EXPIRATION DATE AND, IF AVAILABLE, ALSO THE PRODUCTION DATE

Flour does expire and degrade with time, so make sure the flour you're buying is fresh and still within its "best used by" date!

CHAPTER 2

AN ATLAS OF ITALIAN BREADS

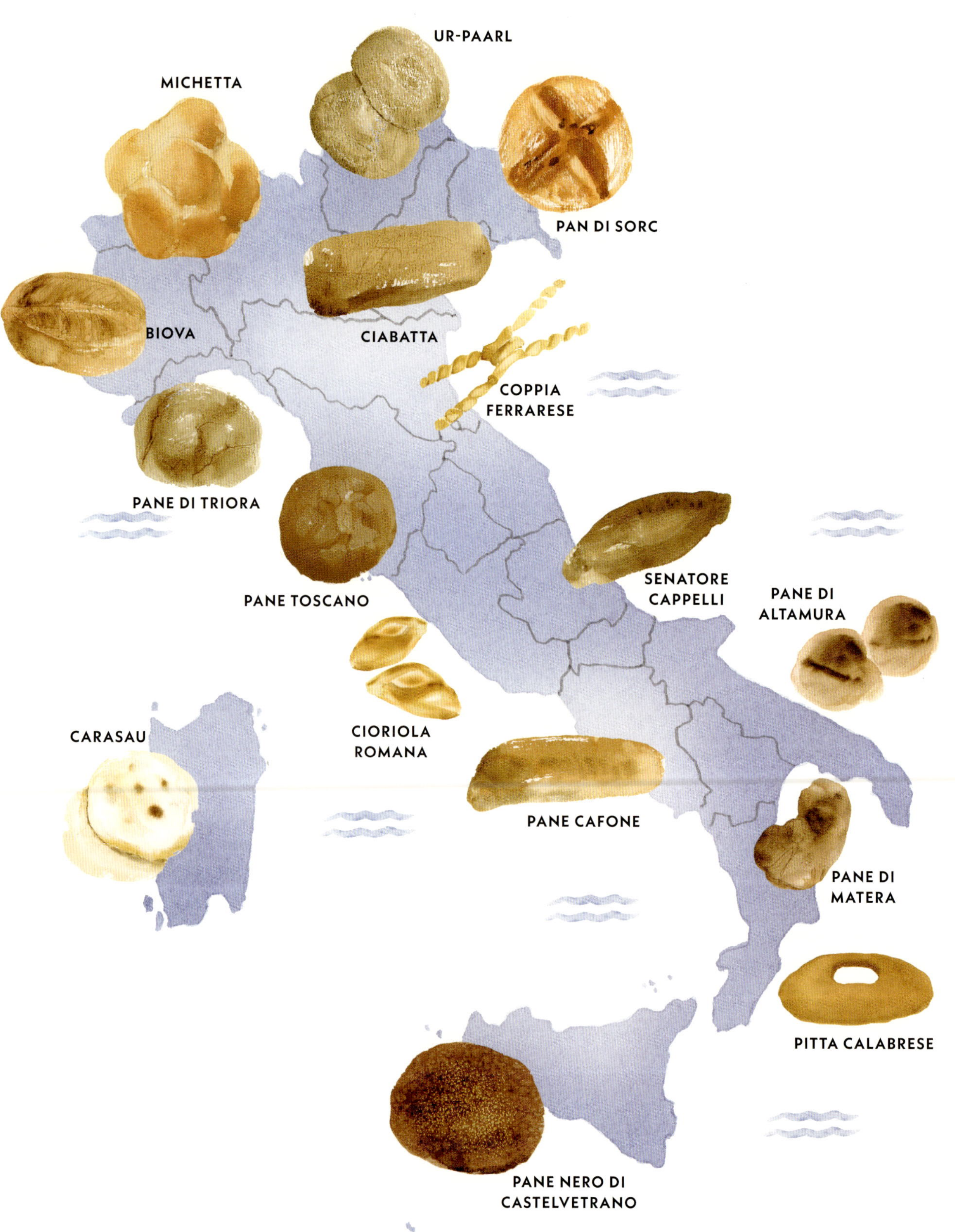
UR-PAARL
MICHETTA
PAN DI SORC
BIOVA
CIABATTA
COPPIA
FERRARESE
PANE DI TRIORA
PANE TOSCANO
SENATORE
CAPPELLI
PANE DI
ALTAMURA
CARASAU
CIORIOLA
ROMANA
PANE CAFONE
PANE DI
MATERA
PITTA CALABRESE
PANE NERO DI
CASTELVETRANO

BREADS OF ITALY

Italy's many breads come in all shapes and flavors. Some are dense, while others are light and fluffy. Each region boasts its own specialties and variations, which you can find in the list below, broken down by region. While many of the *pane*, or bread, types are named after the city where they were created, others highlight a main ingredient. For this reason, the list varies between the traditional Italian names and English translations.

Valle d'Aosta

Miassa
Micoula
Rye bread

Piedmont

Biova
Cariton (or *Caritun*)
Flat breadsticks
Focaccia novarese
Giaco
Grissia
Lingua di suocera
Mica
Monferrina breadsticks
Paisanotta di Druento
Pan Barbarià
Pane di carlo Alberto
Pane nero di Coimo
Panet
Raschietta
Robatà
Rundìtt
Toponin

Liguria

Biova della Val Bormida
Black bread of Pigna
Carpasina
Fisherman's bread
Focaccia di Recco
Focaccia di Voltri
Focaccia Genovese
Gallette
Grissa di Dolceacqua
Herb cake
Libretto
Pane di Triora
Pizzalandrea
Tirà

Lombardy

Baule and *ricciolina*
Bread with figs
Busella
Ciabatta
Corn bread
Luadel di Pomponesco
Miccone Pavese (or *di Stradella)*
Michetta
Pane di Como
Rice bread
Rye bread
Schiacciatina
Schissotto
Tirot di Felonica

Veneto

Bibanesi
Bossolài
Ciopa
Corn bread
Italian ciabatta
Montasù
Pan Biscotto
Piava
Puccia Ladina
Rosetta
Spaccatina
Unleavened bread (matzo)

Trentino

Bechi panzalini
Bina
Cuccalar
Fanzelto
Gramolato
Pan de molche

Alto Adige

Apfelbrot and *palabirabrot*
Bauernpaarl
Breatl
Brezel
Fela strunz
Pindl
Schüttelbrot
Schwarzer weggen
Segalino
Ur-Paarl
Vinschgauer struzn

Friuli-Venezia Giulia

Biga servolana
Bread with corn cracklings
Brown bread
Cornetto istriano
Corn bread
Grispolenta
Pan di sorc
Rosetta or kaiser

Emilia-Romagna

Batarò
Borlengo
Coppia ferrarese
Crescentina (tigella)
Crescentina fritta
Crocetta piacentina
Gnocco ingrassato
Miseria
Pane del bollo
Pane di Pavullo
Piadina romagnola
Potato bread
Pumpkin bread
Stria

Tuscany

Biscotto salato di Roccalbenga
Bozza pratese
Ciaccino
Ficattola
Focaccetta di Aulla
Focaccia di Pasqua salata di Pitigliano
Garfagnana potato bread
Garfagnana spelt bread
Marocca di Casola
Moroccan bread from Montignoso
Neccio
Ottofile corn bread
Pane di Montegemoli
Pane di Po, Signano e Agnino
Pane di Vinca
Pane neccio della Garfagnana
Panigaccio di Podenzana
Panina gialla aretina
Rosemary bread
Schiaccia maremmana
Semelle
Testarolo artigianale pontremolese
Testarolo della Lunigiana
Tuscan bread

Umbria

Ciammella di Itieli
Easter pizza
Homestyle bread
Lumachella
Pan caciato
Pan nociato
Pane di Strettura
Pane di Terni
Torta al testo

Marche

Crescia maceratese
Crostolo del Montefeltro
Farro bread
Homemade loaf
Pane di Chiaserna
Stuffed focaccia
Whole wheat loaf

Abruzzo

Corn bread
Herringbone bread
Pane di senatore Cappelli
Pizza scima
Strozzacavallo

Molise

Taralli di Venafro

Lazio

Aniseed Ciambella from Sambuci
Ciambella a ccancello di Mentana
Ciambella serronese
Ciambella sorana
Ciambellone di Sant'Antonio
Ciriola romana
Fàlia
Flame pizza
Genzano homemade bread
Ju salvaticu
Pamparito di Vignanello
Pane di Lariano
Pane di Salisano
Pane di Velletri
Pane di Vicovaro
Pane giallo di Allumiere
Pani caserecci dei Monti Lepini
Roman white pizza

Campania

Bread with cracklings
Fisherman's bread
Neapolitan bun
Pane cafone
Pane di Padula
Pane di Vallo
Parruozzo
Pizza
Puccellato rustico
Saraolla rye bread
Struppolo
Taralli
Tòrtano

Basilicata

Biscotti a otto
Carchiola
Ciambella
Ficcilatidd' (or *piccilatiedd'*)
Pane di Matera
Pane di Rivello
Pastizz 'rtunnar
Scarcella pomaricana
Strazzata di Avigliano
Stuffed pizzas
Varone

Puglia

Altamura bread
Calzone with young onions
Farrata di Manfredonia
Focaccia a libro di Sammichele di Bari
Pane di Laterza
Pane di Monte Sant'Angelo
Pane garganico
Pettole
Potato bread
Puccia
Scèblasti di Zollino
Taralli

Calabria

Bread with jujubes
Buccellato di Serra San Bruno
Calabrese pitta
Chestnut bread
Cuddura
Filone
Fiscottino
Fraguni calabresi di Pasqua
Frese or *friselle*
Pane di Canolo
Pane di Cerchiara
Pane di Cutro
Pane di Mangone
Pane di Pellegrina
Pitt'ajima
Pizzata
Potato bread
Scaddateddha
Wheat bread

Sicily

Beer bread
Black bread of Castelvetrano
Bukë
Cucciddatu
Cucciddatu di carrozza
Cudduruni di Lentini
Hard loaf bread
Muffoletta
Pane di Monreale
Pane tradizionale di Lentini
Pani di Salemi
Pè
Pupu cu l'ovu
Rianata
Scacciata
Sfincione
Sfoglio ragusano
Vastedda di Enna

Sardinia

Bread with cracklings
Bread with ricotta
Bread with tomato
Civraxu
Coccoi
Moddizzosu
Pà Punyat
Pane Carasau
Pane Pillu
Pistoccu
Spianada
Spianata di Orzieri
Tunda

While you've just seen the hundreds of variations of Italian breads, overall the breads of Italy can be grouped into four main categories that, leaving aside the flavored breads, provide a good basis for choosing or preparing our own loaves.

Hard Dough Breads

This is a type of bread that is characterized by the small amount of water in the dough, around 40 percent, with at most 55 percent hydration. We find these in the North and South. In the North, we have many varieties prepared with common wheat flour: An example is *Ferrarese coppia*, one of the breads I like to call "artistic." In the South and the islands, hard dough breads are prepared with durum wheat semolina, for example, *coccoi* or some Sicilian votive breads. These breads have very smooth crusts and very dense crumbs and can be kept for long periods, not remaining as soft as traditional bread but becoming drier. They are often dried and used as ceremonial or votive breads.

Large Durum Wheat Breads from the South

All the large-size breads that we traditionally find in Central and Southern Italy belong to this family. *Altamura* bread in Basilicata, *Matera* bread in Puglia, and Castelvetrano black bread in Sicily are examples now known outside the region.

These breads were made first by peasants. Their large size means they could bake for a long time in wood-burning ovens and their thick crusts meant they would keep for weeks. In addition, durum wheat was used, which ensures a longer shelf life due to its ability to absorb more water and slow down staling. In order to bake bread, it was often necessary to go to the public bakery or to the village baker. Baking was not a daily activity for individual households. Each bread was mixed and kneaded by hand with the help of the whole family, taken to bake, and a supply of loaves that were good for a sufficiently long time were brought back.

Whole Grain Mountain Breads

Very similar in tradition to the durum wheat breads of the South, whole grain mountain breads originate in mountainous areas and are made from the typical cereals of those altitudes: rye, barley, common wheat, and even corn. They are almost exclusively whole grain breads, as, by tradition, no part of the grain was wasted. The cereal or cereals were cleaned and taken to the mill, where they were ground in their entirety, keeping even the bran, which, due to its fiber content, ensured a longer shelf life. There are rye breads in the Italian mountains that are able to keep for many months. Shelf life was very important because in the inaccessible mountainous areas it was very difficult to reach ovens, especially in the cold months. Bread had to keep for the whole season. Often these loaves were made with a mix of flours that depended on what was grown. Piedmont's *barbarià* bread, for example, is made with common wheat and rye that were once sown at the same time in the field, then milled and baked together.

Panini

Panini, meaning "small loaves of bread," are of a more recent origin. They are not to be confused with sandwiches (the Italian word is the same: *panini*). The two are, however, intertwined. The latter have an older origin: Cutting two slices of a bread and stuffing them created a sandwich even before the 20th century. Small breads, or buns, on the other hand, are shapes that originated in the last century and became popular after World War II. They are products of the affluence that came to the cities and followed the spread of bread-forming machinery. That's when wonders like the *rosetta*, *ciriola*, or *ciabatta* that are filled with the finest local ingredients emerge. These forms often have the same characteristics: white flours or semolina, brewer's yeast, direct leavening, thin crusts, and crispy outsides with soft insides (perfect for filling). They have a shorter shelf life than large loaves and are lighter in texture. Of course, we also find whole grain panini, made with preferments or sourdough. The production of small breads in Italy originated, however, in order to produce quick, easy-to-eat loaves.

TYPES OF ITALIAN BREADS

HARD DOUGH BREADS

MONTASÙ

GRISSIA MONFERRINA

CROCETTA PIACENTINA

COPPIA FERRARESE

BIOVA

MICCONE PAVESE

BUSELLA

PANE DI PAVULLO

PANINI/ BUNS

CIABATTA

KAISERSEMMEL

MICHETTA

BIGA SERVOLANA

CIRIOLA ROMANA

MUFFOLETTA

SEMELLE

ROSETTA

LIBRETTO LIGURE

WHOLE GRAIN BREADS FROM THE MOUNTAINS

RYE BREAD

PAN BIAVA

UR-PAARL

PANE DI CERCHIARA

BLACK BREAD OF COIMO

PAN DE MOLCHE

PUCCIA

PANE BARBARIÀ

LARGE DURUM WHEAT BREADS OF THE SOUTH

PUGLIAN BREAD

ALTAMURA BREAD

PANE DI MATERA

CASTELVETRANO BLACK BREAD

PAGNOTTA DEL DITTAINO

CUCCIDDATU

PANE DI LATERZE

CIVRAXU

PANE DI SARAGOLLA

CIAMBELLA LUCANA

CUDDURA CALABRESE

PANE DI MONREALE

PANE DI PIANA DEGLI ALBANESI

PIAZZA
DEI
PESCATORI

ONE PIZZA, MANY PIZZAS

There is no such thing as "a pizza." There are *pizzas*. Hidden behind the name of Italy's iconic dish—known all over the world—is a universe of variations and flavors. From the type of dough to the ingredients, and from how it is baked to how it is topped, the landscape of Italian pizzas (including focaccias and flatbreads) is so varied that we can justifiably say whatever city you go to, you will find pizza and focaccia. This is not meant to take anything away from Naples, which brought pizza to world prominence. If you haven't read it yet, I recommend my book *Pizza per tutti* (*Pizza for Everyone*), where I explain that in Italy and around the world there is not just one pizza, but many pizzas, which vary according to local tradition.

Pizzas

We have various round pizzas—pizzeria pizzas, to be precise. First and foremost, there is the Neapolitan pizza, the real thing, which can have different characteristics depending on how it is made and baked: round, contemporary, and so on. Traveling up Italy and moving to the capital, one cannot fail to mention Roman pizza, which is flatter, without edges and very crispy (the *scrocchiarella*, or "crunchy one," as it is called in Rome). Round pizza in Italy can still have many other local versions, depending on the region, the flours used, and the oven temperature. Then there are round pizzas baked in *padellini* (small round pans), a cross between those made in pizzerias and in bakeries, or pizzas that are not round, such as the white Roman pizza (*pizza bianca*), the so-called *pizza alla pala* baked on the refractory stone of the oven, or the Roman *pizza al taglio* (pizza by the slice) that is baked in a pan, topped in different ways, and sold in a classic rectangular format throughout Italy.

Focaccias

You may be wondering what the difference is between pizza and focaccia. Pizza is made to rise, then rolled out, perhaps topped, and then put directly into the oven; focaccia, on the other hand, undergoes a final rise in a baking pan before going into the oven.

Speaking of focaccia, in Italy we have incredible wonders that are almost always the offspring not of pizza makers but of bakers: the focaccia from Liguria, the focaccia with cherry tomatoes from Puglia (and its many variations), the Tuscan *schiacciata*, and the Palermo *sfincione*, just to name a few examples.

Flatbreads

They are not always made with yeast, and they are not always baked in a real oven, but nonetheless they are part of the category of breads. There are, for example, the *piadina* from Romagna, the *torta al testo*, the *crescia* from the Marche region, and we can include the *farinata* and *cecina*, prepared with chickpea flour and typical of the Tyrrhenian coast, from Liguria to Tuscany, but which we find in a similar recipe in Sicily, the delicious *panelle*, to be enjoyed plain or stuffed in a bun.

TYPES OF ITALIAN FLATBREADS

ROMAN PIZZA BY THE SLICE

RIANATA TRAPANESE

PAN PIZZA

PIZZAS

ROUND ITALIAN PIZZA

ROMAN PADDLE PIZZA

TRUE NEAPOLITAN PIZZA

SFINCIONE

GENOVESE

BARESE

ABRUZZESE FLATBREAD

FOCACCIAS

DI RECCO

TIROT MANTOVANO

BRUSADELA ROMAGNESE

SCHIACCIATA TOSCANA

SFINCIONE PALERMITANO

PIADINA

FARINATA OR CECINA

FLATBREADS

TORTA AL TESTO

CRESCIA MARCHIGIANA

PANELLE

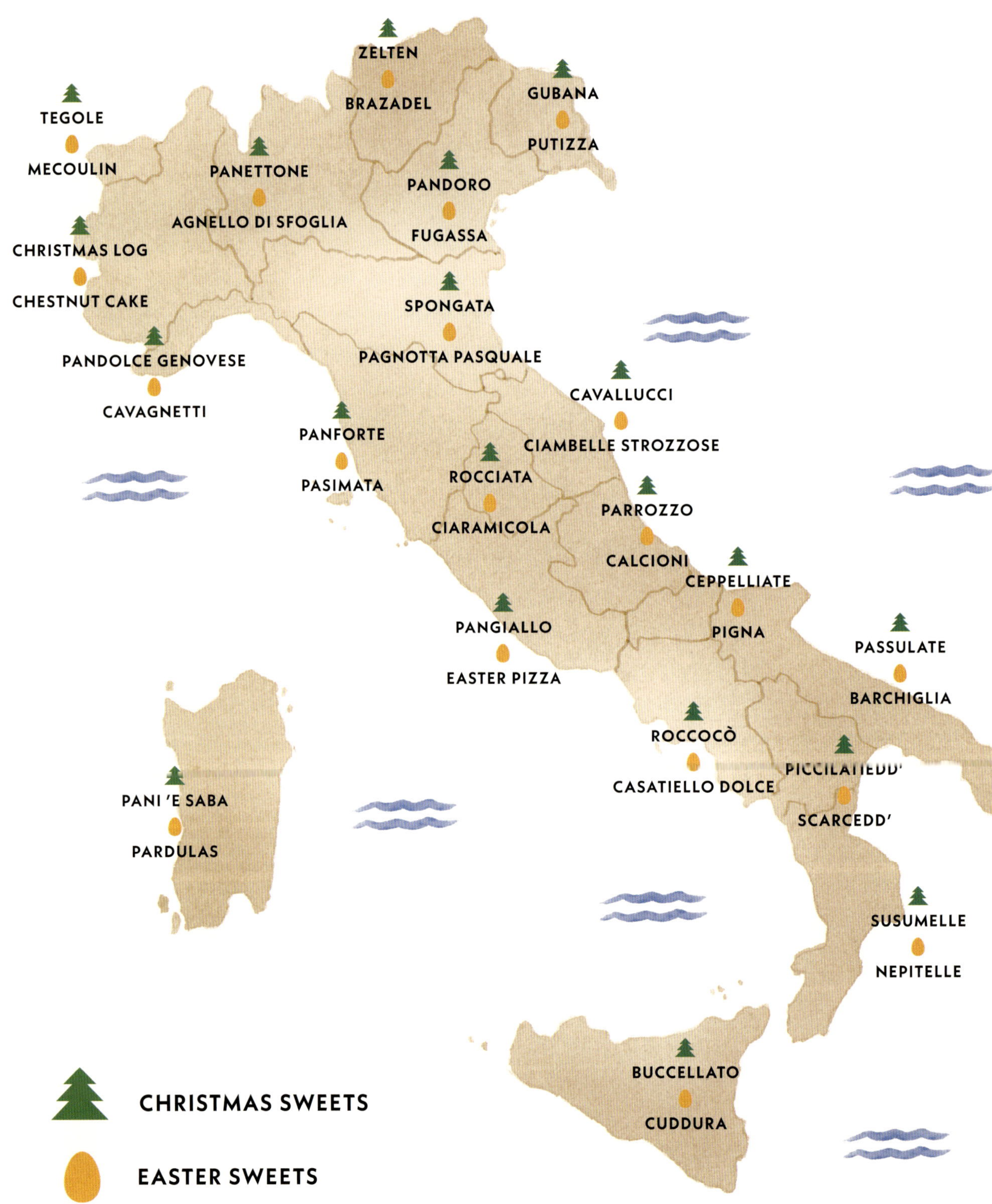

ZELTEN
BRAZADEL
GUBANA
PUTIZZA
TEGOLE
MECOULIN
PANETTONE
AGNELLO DI SFOGLIA
PANDORO
FUGASSA
CHRISTMAS LOG
CHESTNUT CAKE
SPONGATA
PAGNOTTA PASQUALE
PANDOLCE GENOVESE
CAVAGNETTI
CAVALLUCCI
CIAMBELLE STROZZOSE
PANFORTE
PASIMATA
ROCCIATA
CIARAMICOLA
PARROZZO
CALCIONI
CEPPELLIATE
PIGNA
PANGIALLO
EASTER PIZZA
PASSULATE
BARCHIGLIA
ROCCOCÒ
CASATIELLO DOLCE
PICCILATIEDD'
SCARCEDD'
PANI 'E SABA
PARDULAS
SUSUMELLE
NEPITELLE
BUCCELLATO
CUDDURA
CHRISTMAS SWEETS
EASTER SWEETS

HOLIDAY SWEETS

Along with breads and pizzas, mouthwatering sweets also come out of the oven, and how can this not be mentioned in a book celebrating Italy's culinary biodiversity? Every saint and every village has its own typical recipes, many of which are baked for the holidays, first and foremost Christmas and Easter. You will find a brief roundup of some of the best-known sweet traditions on the opposite page.

Christmas

In a triumph of spices, and dried and candied fruits, there are many traditional sweets that characterize the holiday table. The quintessential Christmas argument in Italy, however, is always the same: *panettone*, Lombard by tradition, or *pandoro*, attributed to the Veneto region. There are those who cannot give up the raisins and candied fruit of the former and those who are crazy about the buttery, vanilla flavor of the latter. You can find a recipe for *panettone* on page 234. But the Christmas leavened goods certainly do not end there. Continuing a quick tour of Italy, we find in Piedmont the *tronchetto di Natale* (Christmas log), a soft sponge cake rolled and topped with cream, reminiscent of the shape of a log; on the sweetened breads front, there is the Friulian *gubana*, a dough spiral made with dried fruit and grappa (an Italian spirit). In Liguria, *pandolce* is the star, while in Tuscany it's not a holiday without *panforte*. In Abruzzo's *parrozzo* we find Lazio's *pangiallo*, which gets its name from the color of the yellow icing that covers it. There is no shortage of classic Christmas cakes often prepared with dried fruit, including *zelten* from Trentino, *spongata* from Emilia-Romagna, and *barchiglia* from Puglia.

Also worth mentioning are cookies prepared for the holidays, such as *roccocò*, *susumelle*, and *ceppeliate*, and sweet rolls, such as Pugliese *passulate* and Sardinian *pani 'e saba*.

Easter

From North to South (and in fact it does not appear on the map here because it is difficult to give it a regional location), the star of Easter is undoubtedly the *colomba*, the leavened cake shaped like a dove and covered with a mouthwatering almond glaze. Among the leavened treats popular at Easter, we also have the Valdostan *mecoulin*, the Venetian *fugassa*, the Triestine *putizza* (like the *gubana*, shaped like a snail), the Romagna Easter loaf, the Garfagnana *pasimata*, and the Easter pizza in its many variations that include the *pigna* in Ciociaria and the sweet *casatiello* from Campania. The Ligurian *cavagnetti* are reminiscent of a basket, while the Sardinian *pardulas* are filled with ricotta cheese and the Calabrian *nepitelle* are filled with chocolate and dried fruit. The Trentino *brazadel* and Marche's *strozzose ciambelle* look like small doughnuts and are always prepared in single portions, which are also convenient for an Easter picnic.

FUOCOFARINA

CHAPTER 3

ITALIAN SOURDOUGHS: A COMPLETE GUIDE

A PRACTICAL APPROACH TO SOURDOUGH

There is no such thing as a sourdough, there are sourdoughs.

I have talked many times about sourdough, how to refresh it and use it depending on the end product you want to achieve. In this book, I would like to provide further clarity and deal with the subject in a comprehensive way and with a practical approach, starting with what exactly different sourdoughs have in common.

What Is It?

Sourdough is a dough made from flour and water in varying proportions, which must be left to ferment at room temperature so that it can spontaneously produce a full-fledged population of microorganisms, causing the mixture to become sour (which is why it is called sourdough). Fermentation results from the presence of yeasts (fungi) and lactic acid bacteria, which cooperate with each other and allow the natural yeast to develop. These live and proliferate if fed consistently through the addition of water and flour. This is "refreshment," or "feeding," the secret to a quality sourdough starter because it serves to keep the dough alive and healthy.

Yeasts are responsible for alcoholic fermentation, which occurs under anaerobic conditions (absence of oxygen) and consists of the process of converting glucose and fructose into carbon dioxide and ethyl alcohol. These sugars, called fermentable sugars, are available in flour only in a very small part (about 2 percent), while the vast majority is present in the form of starches (complex sugars). Therefore, the role of enzymes, which break down the complex sugar molecules into simpler parts directly usable by yeasts, is essential. The enzymes responsible for this function are alpha-amylase, beta-amylase and glucoamylase, which are found naturally in flours and work in concert, one after the other in the order given, converting starches into glucose and activating the moment water is inserted. This last process preceding alcoholic fermentation is what is known as maturation, or the preparation of food for the yeasts by the enzymes.

It is the bacteria that initiate lactic fermentation. They are present both in the flour and in the surrounding environment. This is the reason why, even using the same recipe, you may have small (or large) differences depending on the place of production. Different types of acids are obtained from lactic fermentation, giving the final product distinct characteristics. Lactic acid has a sweet, non-bitter taste that gives recipes the typical taste of yogurt or well-fermented flour. Acetic acid, on the other hand, which is produced in small amounts during fermentation, is what can be detected when smelling a yeast product and experiencing a note that may be reminiscent of vinegar. It is very important that this component always outnumber the lactic component, otherwise the products would taste distinctly sour and sometimes even bitter.

Why Use It?

There is no question that sourdough, whether at home or in a professional kitchen, can be challenging. It requires knowledge, experience, and time, not to mention the fact that the results are not always equal (brewer's yeast is easier to master and you will still find it in many recipes). Working with a living, ever-evolving material, however, is exciting and a source of great satisfaction.

There are many advantages of using sourdough. The first benefit has to do with digestibility. Thanks to the presence of *lactobacilli* and the long fermentation time, complex proteins are transformed into amino acids, molecules that are simpler and more digestible. Sourdough also greatly reduces levels of phytic acid, an antinutrient substance that prevents us from assimilating elements in flours such as iron, calcium, and zinc that are important to our bodies. Products made with sourdough also have a longer shelf life and their crumbs tend to remain fluffy and soft for longer. Especially in large breads, the acidic environment created during fermentation inhibits the formation of mold and microorganisms that are harmful to health, and slows down what is called starch retrogradation, a process that increases the product's staling.

The Importance of Temperature

You should know that temperature greatly influences the action of a sourdough starter. In the range between 32°F and 39°F (0°C and 4°C), the activity of bacteria and yeasts is inhibited; above 39°F (4°C) the yeasts start working, albeit very slowly, while the lactic acid bacteria show no signs of life at least until 53°F to 57°F (12°C to 14°C). Beyond that threshold, they start working again and up to 82°F to 86°F (28°C to 30°C) produce both lactic and acetic acid. Above 86°F (30°C), some bacteria slow down their activity, while yeasts reach maximum viability around 95°F (35°C).

The beneficial aspects do not end there, as products made with sourdough have a lower glycemic index than those made with brewer's yeast, because the acidity in the dough allows a slower release of glucose into the bloodstream during digestion.

Lastly, sourdough positively influences the flavor and aroma profile of products containing it. In fact, the prolonged action of particular enzymes, activated by the interaction between yeast and lactic acid bacteria, "unpack" the proteins in the dough, resulting in the formation of compounds, volatile and otherwise, that impart a more intense and complex taste and aroma during baking.

HOW TO MAKE IT

To create sourdough from scratch, it is necessary to trigger fermentation. I always follow the same method, regardless of the type of yeast I want to obtain (e.g., liquid or solid). I use a whole grain flour, usually rye flour because it is the one that, in my experience, has the greatest fermentation power. The process takes about four weeks; from week five on, you can start refreshing it.

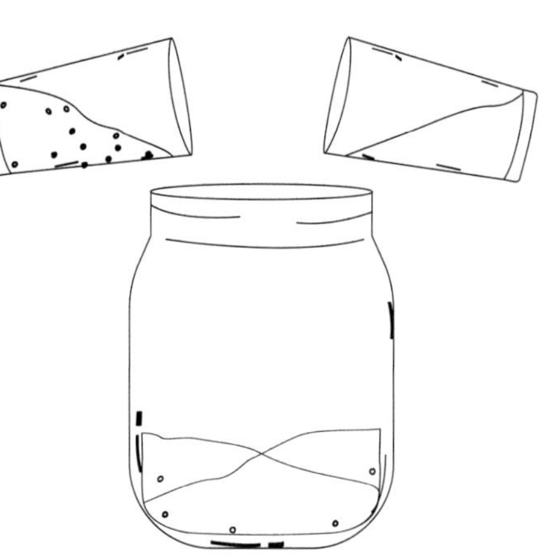

DAY ONE

Mix 100 g of whole grain rye flour and 100 ml of warm water (86°F–95°F [30°C–35°C]) in a jar to make a thick batter.

Cover with sterile gauze and secure with a rubber band.

Let it rest for 48 hours at room temperature.

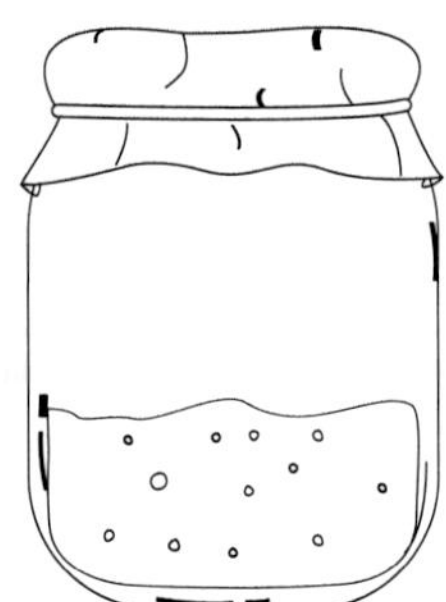

DAY THREE

Check to see if microbubbles have formed. If none have formed, start over.

Remove and discard half of the resulting yeast and refresh the rest by adding warm water and rye flour in a 1:1:1 ratio.

Stir, cover, and let stand for another 48 hours at room temperature.

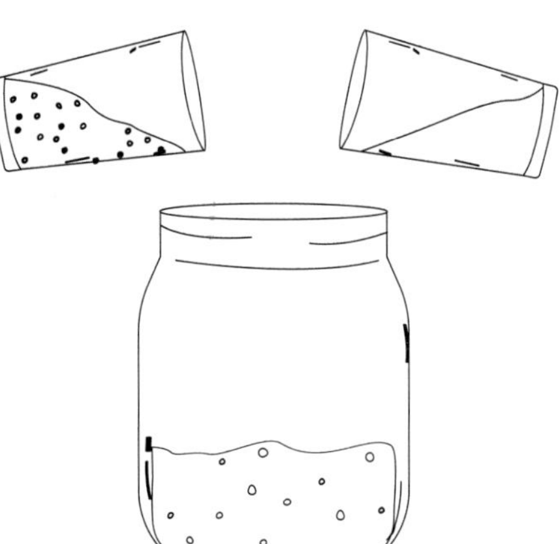

DAY FIVE

Check for bubbles. If none, start again from the beginning.

Take 100 g of sourdough starter, discarding the rest, and repeat the refreshment as you did in the second step, then cover and let rest for another 48 hours at room temperature.

DAY SEVEN

Take 100 g of sourdough starter, discarding the rest, and refresh it again with equal measurements of water and flour.

Mix, cover, and let it rest for another 48 hours at room temperature.

At this stage, the yeast will almost double in volume and you will begin to smell more fermentation.

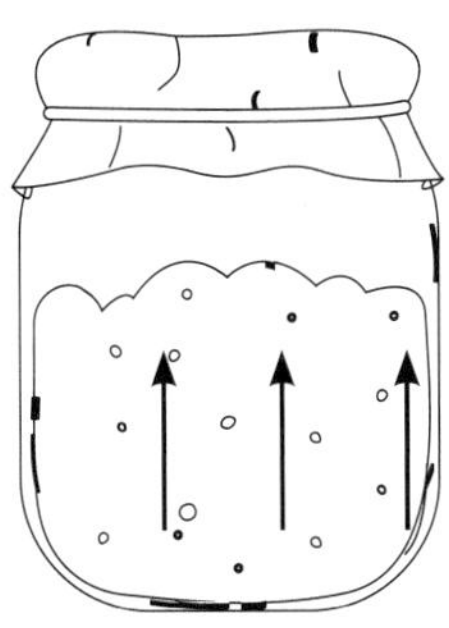

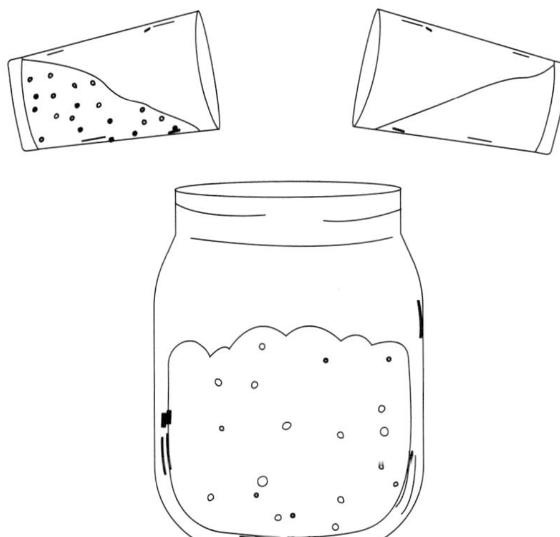

WEEK TWO

The yeast should be refreshed daily in the same proportions and will double in volume after 3 to 4 hours at room temperature.

The mixture will likely smell like yogurt or fresh flour.

WEEK THREE

If all goes well, you can store the sourdough starter in the refrigerator, remembering to refresh it at least three times a week.

For the refreshment, you can substitute one part of whole grain rye flour with white whole wheat or first clear flour.

WEEK FOUR

The yeast is ready to be used and can also be refreshed with white whole wheat or first clear flour alone.

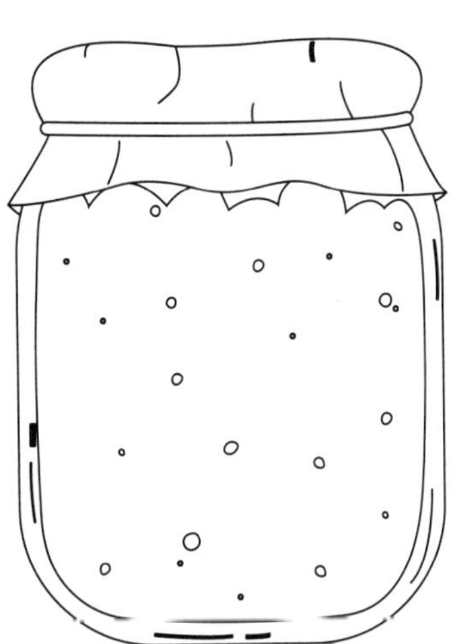

To keep the sourdough starter alive and enhance its fermentative capacity, it needs to be refreshed.

Now that we know how to make the sourdough starter, we can focus on how to keep it alive and the factors that determine its quality, namely the flour, water, environment, and temperature.

It is important that the flour used to refresh the yeast be as natural as possible. Choose an organic flour so that it does not have pesticide residues, herbicides, or other substances that can go on to kill or weaken the population of microorganisms. As for type and strength, the intended use of the yeast should be taken into consideration. If it is to be used for making *panettone* and *colomba* breads, for example, it is best to refresh it with a very strong flour, while if it is intended for bread making, it is best to go for a flour that is less strong but has a higher fiber content, such as type 2 common wheat flour (white whole wheat in the United States). Keep in mind, however, that it will tend to ferment faster and may develop more acidity compared to a more refined flour.

Another very important element is water. For it to promote bacterial growth, it should not be too loaded with mineral salts.

Be careful with cleaning products because they inhibit the proliferation of bad bacteria, but they also kill good microorganisms. I recommend that you wash what you need with warm water and, at most, use diluted 95 percent alcohol. Also avoid storing your sourdough starter near cheese or deli meats.

Don't forget that sourdough lives well at temperatures between 68°F and 95°F (20°C and 35°C), but if you can't refresh it and use it every day, it's best to store it in the refrigerator.

Refreshing Sourdough

In order to keep the sourdough starter alive and enhance its fermentative capacity, it is necessary to refresh it, that is, to add water and flour in varying proportions. During this process, a kind of natural selection helps ensure that only the best yeast and bacteria remain. Refreshing also serves to lower the degree of acidity of the dough, and for this reason, it is ideal to do it once a day.

There are many schools of thought on how to do this, and each is valid depending on the use and the end product. In general, I recommend that you use an amount of flour that is never less than the amount of yeast to be refreshed. Basically, if we have 100 g of yeast to refresh, we need to add at least 100 g of flour. The amount of water, on the other hand, depends on the type of yeast and is always calculated based on the amount of flour added to the refresher: It can range from 45 to 100 percent (45 g of water for every 100 g of flour).

Another key aspect is the final temperature of the yeast after refreshment. Yeast and bacteria work well around 82°F to 86°F (28°C to 30°C), and it is ideal to work with a water temperature in that range. (The water temperature should never exceed 115°F [46°C], because that will kill the yeast.) Keep in mind that other variables—including the room temperature, the temperature of the yeast to be refreshed, the temperature of the flour, and the temperature of the mixer—will either cool off or warm up the temperature of the yeast as it refreshes. If these variables tend to be under the ideal 82°F to 86°F (28°C to 30°C) temperature range in your work environment, use a water temperature at the upper end of that range.

Solid Sourdough Starter

A solid sourdough starter, also called mother dough, is one of the most common sourdough starters used by home cooks. It should not be confused with the carry-over dough or *criscito* that our Italian grandparents often used, because carry-over dough consists of portions of dough taken and used as starters in subsequent breadmaking. Mother dough, on the other hand, is a real yeast that is kept alive with continuous refreshments.

HOW TO REFRESH IT

The classic method calls for an amount of flour equal to the starting yeast, while the water typically varies from 50 to 60 percent of the weight of the flour.

Since, compared to other types, sourdough tends to give products a more acidic taste, I recommend refreshing it by doubling the amount of flour compared to the starting yeast.

Example

100 g of sourdough + 200 g of flour + 100 g to 120 g of water

HOW TO USE IT

After refreshment, place the sourdough in a container—I use a tall, narrow measuring pitcher—and let it rest at a temperature of 77°F to 86°F (25°C to 30°C). When it doubles in volume, it is ready to be used in an amount ranging from 10 to 40 percent of the amount of flour, depending on the recipe.

HOW TO STORE IT

I recommend that you refresh the yeast every day with the 1:2 ratio (twice the amount of flour to the amount of yeast and flour and 50 percent water to flour) leave it 2 hours at room temperature and store it in the refrigerator immediately afterward. If you prefer to keep it in the refrigerator for several days, it is better to use one part yeast and three parts flour (100 g of yeast, 300 g of flour, and 150 g to 180 g of water). In this way, you can keep it sealed in a container with a lid or with food wrap for a week, after which you will need to refresh it.

When you are ready to use it, you must remove it from the refrigerator, refresh it as described, and wait until it doubles in volume.

Liquid Cultured Yeast

Liquid cultured yeast, also known as liquid sourdough, is what I use most for making breads, flat-breads, and pizzas, to which it imparts a slightly acidic, almost sweet flavor. I find it to be an easy-to-manage yeast, because all it takes to refresh it is a jar and a spoon. It is also easy to control because, when stored in a measuring pitcher or tall, narrow jar, it is easy to see the volume it develops during fermentation.

HOW TO REFRESH IT

Standard refreshment is very simple, as it involves the same amounts of yeast, flour, and water.

> ***Example***
>
> 100 g of liquid yeast + 100 g of flour + 100 g of water

HOW TO USE IT

Once refreshed, the yeast should be placed in a container that can hold three times the volume of the starting yeast. Then cover it with plastic wrap and let it rise at 86°F (30°C) until it doubles in volume (if needed, you can use the oven as a leavening chamber). If you want to prepare it the day before, however, leave it 2 hours at 86°F (30°C) and then transfer it to the refrigerator. After 24 hours, you can use it directly after taking it out of the refrigerator.

The amount of yeast to use inside the doughs ranges from 10 to 40 percent of the weight of the flour, depending on the recipe (usually the standard amount is 25 to 30 percent).

HOW TO STORE IT

I recommend that you refresh the yeast with twice the amount of flour and water and refrigerate it immediately after refreshment. This way you can store it for a week, after which you will need to refresh it again.

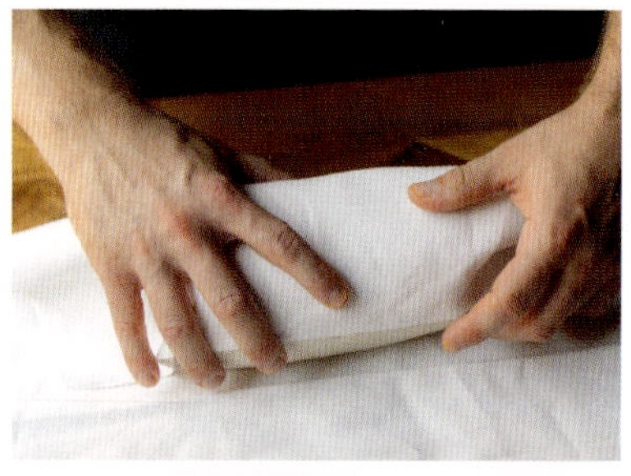

Strained Yeast (Milanese)

Also known as the traditional Milanese method, strained yeast is usually used in the production of large, leavened goods such as *panettone* and *colomba*. It requires a great deal of perseverance and is quite labor-intensive: After refreshing, it is necessary to roll it out with a rolling pin, since a sheeter is usually used at the professional level. I do not recommend it for home use, but it may be interesting to see what results can be achieved.

Putting the yeast "under pressure" inside a bag causes it to develop greater vitality and, excluding the first stages of leavening, it will act without oxygen, favoring the production of lactic acid at the expense of acetic acid: For this reason, products made with this type of yeast keep very long.

HOW TO REFRESH IT

The yeast should be refreshed with one part yeast, two parts flour, and 45 percent water on the added flour; then it should be placed in a cloth and tied (as pictured).

> ***Example***
>
> 100 g yeast + 200 g flour + 90 g water

HOW TO USE IT

Ideally, you should let it rest for 16 to 18 hours at 61°F to 64°F (16°C to 18°C). Since this temperature is difficult to replicate at home, you can also store it in the refrigerator for 24 hours at 39°F (4°C). After this time, if you want to make bread you need to remove the yeast from the bag, remove the outermost crust, take only the middle part, and refresh it by adding equal weight of flour and 50 percent water. It is then allowed to rise in a warm place (79°F to 82°F [26°C to 28°C]) in a tall, narrow container until the volume has tripled. To make a panettone, on the other hand, it is necessary to do three refreshments, with the same amount of flour and 45 percent water.

HOW TO STORE IT

After use, a refresh should be made (one part yeast, two parts flour, and 45 percent water to the weight of flour), roll the yeast with a rolling pin, put it back in the tightly sealed bag, and store it in the refrigerator, where it can remain for up to a week before being refreshed another time.

Piedmontese Water Bath Method

This is similar to the Milanese method, with the big difference being that instead of putting it tightly bound in a bag, the yeast is coiled like a snail shell and placed in a container filled with water (which must weigh three times as much as the yeast). This method, like the previous one, is used mainly in the professional world.

In water, the acidity is slightly discharged, the yeast retains a "sweeter" flavor, and, as a result, products containing it do not tend to develop marked sour notes.

HOW TO REFRESH IT

One part yeast, two parts flour, and 45 percent water are always used.

HOW TO USE IT

The yeast should be left to rest in water for 16 to 18 hours at 61°F to 64°F (16°C to 18°C). You can keep it in the refrigerator (near 39°F [4°C]) for 24 hours.

After this time has passed, if you want to make bread you need to remove it from the water, refresh it with equal weight of flour and 40 percent water, let it rise in a warm place (79°F to 82°F [26°C to 28°C]) inside a tall, narrow container, and wait for it to triple in volume.

To make a panettone, on the other hand, you need to do three refreshments, with the same amount of flour and 45 percent water.

HOW TO STORE IT

After using it, you need to refresh it (one part yeast, two parts flour, and 45 percent water to the weight of the flour), roll the yeast with a rolling pin, and put it back into the water inside the container (one part yeast and three parts water). It can be kept in the refrigerator for 4 or 5 days. After this time, it is necessary to refresh it, as the yeast could dissolve in the water.

How to Store Yeast for Long Periods

If we cannot use our yeast for an extended period—because we are absent or simply do not have time—but do not want to throw it away, it is advisable to pulverize it.

For solid yeast, such as Milanese and Piedmontese yeast or sourdough, simply crumble it into small pieces and refresh it by adding equal weights of yeast and flour. Then, using a stand mixer, make a second refreshment with just the flour, without water, to obtain a powdery mixture that can be transferred to an airtight bag and stored in the refrigerator for up to 6 months. The important thing is that the yeast be well mixed and dry. If we want to be more certain, we can spread the powder in a baking pan and let it dry well in the oven with the light on for a few hours, being careful to keep the temperature always below 95°F (35°C).

To pulverize liquid cultured yeast, the procedure is the same, but in the refreshment, you need to keep a ratio of 1:2 (twice the amount of flour to yeast). To use the pulverized yeast again, simply put it in the mixer, add the water from the refreshment that was left out, and run the mixer until the desired consistency is reached; there may be some lumps at first, but they will tend to disappear as the days go by.

It will take at least three refreshments with doubling in volume before the yeast can be used again. It is important to be aware that the doubling time will be decidedly slow during the first few days (it may take up to 24 hours) and that the yeast should always be kept at room temperature during this revival phase.

In case you need to store the powdered yeast for more than 6 months (not more than a year) you can follow the same procedure but, when finished, store it in the freezer. At the time of use, you should move the frozen yeast to the refrigerator for 24 hours before refreshing at room temperature. Keep in mind, however, that the yeast will be much "sleepier" and it may take about 10 days to bring it back to normal conditions.

CHAPTER 4

THE BASIC ITALIAN DOUGHS

PERFECTION FROM PRACTICE

Practice the following preparations and you will discover how many small differences can become fundamental details.

Once you have learned how to choose the most suitable flours for what you are baking—understanding the cereals from which they come, how they are selected, and how they have been processed—and how to orient yourself, with well-defined rules, I think it's appropriate to pause and gain a little experience with some basic doughs, so that you can then adapt them to whatever you want to make.

These are recipes that will come in handy on many occasions, perhaps when you want to bake something simple, without too much processing. In my opinion, these are the perfect breads to start with. What's more, you'll effortlessly make them again and again. They include some of the many types of breadmaking that are the stars of Italy's biodiversity that I told you about in the first part of the book: common wheat breads (you'll find a step-by-step recipe for *filone*), durum wheat breads (a classic loaf) and mountain breads (a rye bread), a base for a pan pizza that you can top according to your own tastes, and a brioche loaf to be eaten for breakfast.

To help you further, I wanted to capture all the steps in the recipe, so that the words are accompanied and explained by photos as well. You will see clearly how to add each ingredient and, in my view especially, how to make the folds when needed and how to shape or weave different parts of dough. If you do not feel like a seasoned baker, this will help you become familiar with a variety of leavened breads and more easily read the next section devoted to the many recipes of our culinary tradition. Practice with the following recipes: You will discover how many small differences can become fundamental details. Quantities of ingredients, right timing, and a good dose of manual dexterity—which must be acquired and practiced—will guarantee you skills that once learned will enthrall you, just as they captivated me as a child, and will never leave you again.

Then you can move on to the next steps: deepen, vary, and even create. But it is always good to start with the basics—that goes for artists, technicians, and those in any kind of work. Eventually experience will come, allowing you to proceed with confidence.

I hope the photos of the various steps will give you a hand, although then it will be your hands that will form small and large wonders, and which lie behind most traditional Italian products.

FILONE DI GRANO TENERO
CLASSIC SOURDOUGH BREAD

Makes 1 medium loaf

INGREDIENTS

50 g white whole wheat flour
330 g water
150 g liquid cultured yeast (see page 77)
12 g salt

1. ❶ ❷ In a large bowl, mix the flour with 300 g of the water. Mix for about 4 minutes, then let the mixture rest for 1 hour at room temperature.
2. ❸ Incorporate the sourdough starter ❹ and continue mixing until the dough is smooth. ❺ Add the salt and remaining 30 g of water and mix again until the dough is nice and smooth ❻.
3. ❼ Cover and let rise in a warm place (ideally, 81°F [27°C]) for 3 hours. The dough will become bubbly and double in size.
4. Transfer the dough to the work surface ❽ and fold it back on itself as shown in photos ❾ ❿ ⓫ ⓬ to form a loaf.
5. ⓭ Let it rise in a well-floured tea towel for 30 minutes at room temperature and then for 12 hours in the refrigerator. ⓮ The dough should be puffy.
6. Preheat the oven 475°F (240°C). Score the top ⓯ and put it in the oven on a baking stone with a baking paddle. Bake for about 45 minutes.

1

2

3

4

5

6

7

8

9

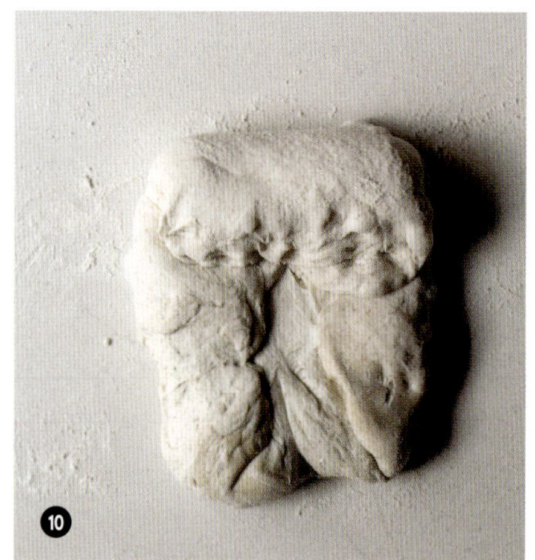
10

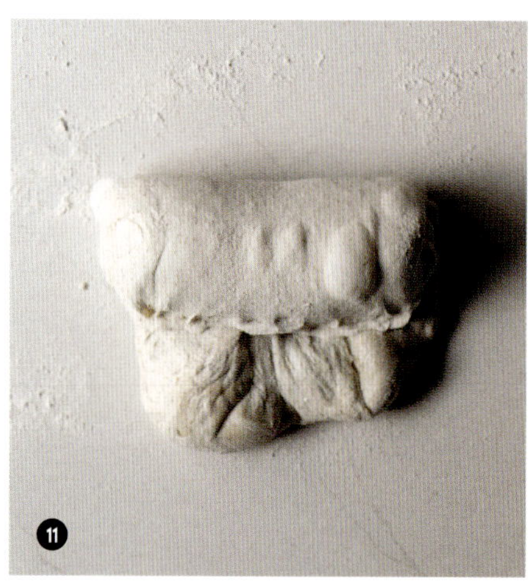
11

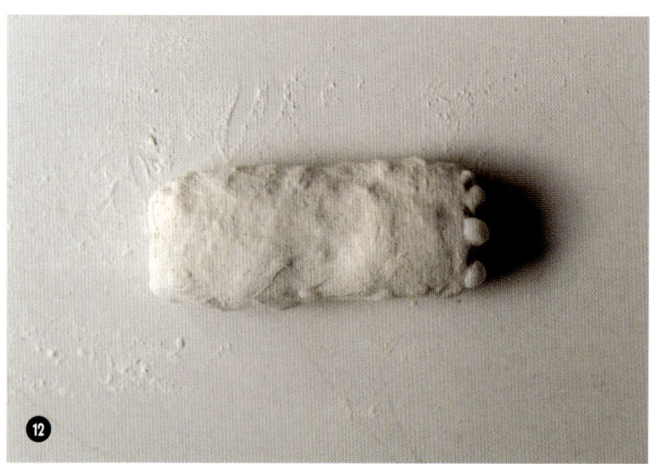
12

13

14

15

PANE DI SEGALE
RYE BREAD

Makes 1 medium round loaf

INGREDIENTS

500 g whole grain rye flour
400 g warm water (105°F [40°C])
100 g solid sourdough starter (see page 76)
12 g salt

1. ❶ ❷ In a large bowl, combine the flour with the warm water. Knead for 2 to 3 minutes, ❸ then incorporate the sourdough starter (if possible, previously refreshed with rye) and knead for about 5 minutes. ❹ ❺ Add the salt and let it be thoroughly absorbed.

2. ❻ Cover and let rest for 40 minutes at room temperature. Generously flour a work surface and roll out the dough. Shape the loaf into a wide round and place it in a well-floured bowl ❼. Let rise in a warm place for another 40 minutes.

3. Preheat the oven to 400°F (200°C). Transfer the bread to a lightly floured or parchment paper–lined baking sheet and bake until deep golden for 45 minutes. The crust should be cracked and the bread should be cooked through.

PAGNOTTA DI GRANO DURO
RUSTIC SOURDOUGH BREAD

Makes 1 large round loaf

INGREDIENTS

500 g hard wheat semolina
370 g cold water
150 g sourdough starter (see page 76)
12 g salt

1. ❶ ❷ In a large bowl, mix the semolina with 320 g of the cold water ❸ and let it rest for 1 hour at room temperature.

2. ❹ Next, add the sourdough starter and mix until the dough is smooth ❺ ❻, then add the salt and the remaining 50 g of water ❼ and work it again so that the dough becomes smooth and silky.

3. ❽ Let it rest for about 2 hours at room temperature.

4. ❾ On a lightly floured work surface, shape the dough into a round loaf following the steps you see in the photo.

5. ❿ Place it in a large bowl, cover with a well-floured tea towel, and let it rise for 1 hour at room temperature and then 12 hours in the refrigerator.

6. ⓫ Turn the loaf upside down on the wooden baking paddle, and make a crosscut with the help of a well-sharpened knife ⓬ ⓭ ⓮. I use a razor blade or a carving knife.

7. Preheat the oven to 475°F (240°C) and bake for 15 minutes. Lower the oven temperature to 410°F (210°C) and continue baking for about 50 minutes, until the crust of the bread is golden in color.

1

2

3

4

5

6

7

8

9

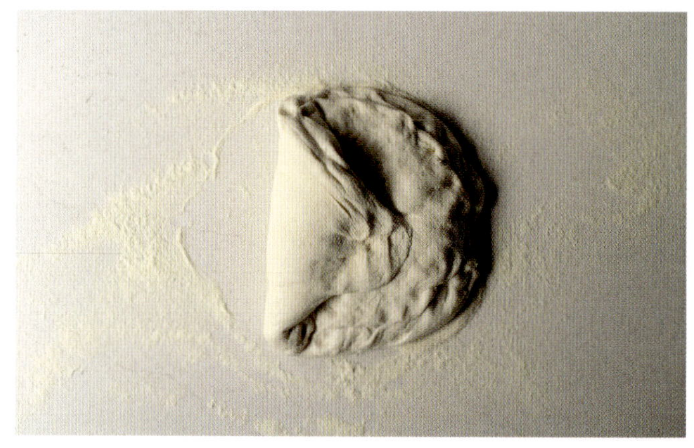

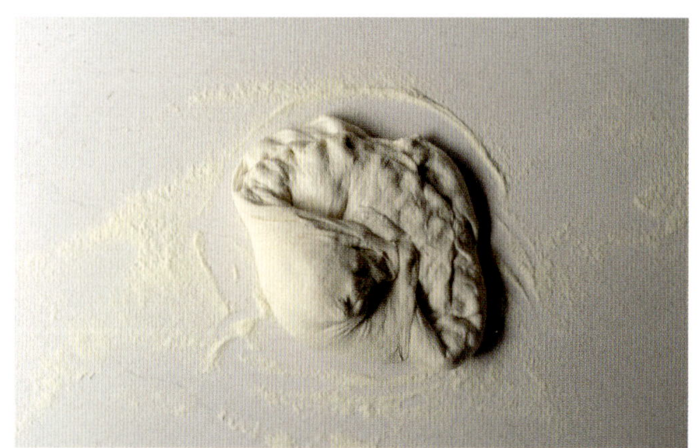

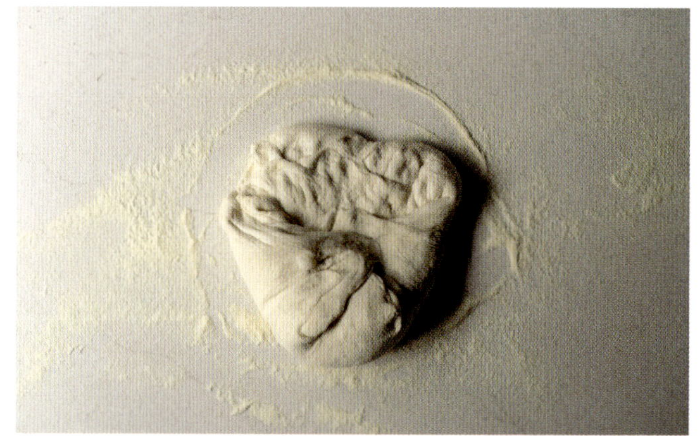

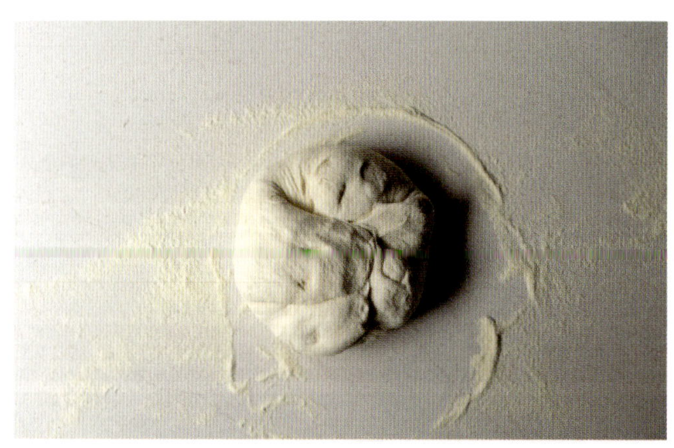

10

11

12

13

14

PAN PIZZA

Makes 1 medium pizza

INGREDIENTS

500 g all-purpose flour
280 g water
5 g fresh brewer's yeast, crumbled
11 g salt
50 g extra virgin olive oil, plus more as needed

1. ❶ Put the flour in a bowl, pour in 260 g of the water, and mix roughly for a few minutes. Let it rest for 10 minutes, ❷ then add the yeast and continue mixing for about 15 minutes, or until you get a uniform dough.

2. ❸ Incorporate the salt and remaining 20 g of water and mix for 10 minutes, ❹ then add the oil and let it be absorbed while still handling the dough.

3. ❺ Let it rest in a lightly oiled bowl, at room temperature, for 2 hours.

4. ❻ Divide the dough into four even mounds.

5. ❼ ❽ Fold the dough rounds back on themselves, ❾ so as to form balls with a smooth, silky surface, ❿ and let rest at room temperature for 1 hour.

6. ⓫ Oil your hands and spread each ball until it reaches the edges of the pan (see Note); if the dough shrinks, stop for 10 to 15 minutes before resuming.

7. ⓬ Let the stretched-out dough rest in the baking pan for about 30 minutes.

8. Preheat the oven to 475°F (240°C). Top the pizza according to your taste and bake, preferably on a baking stone, for 10 to 15 minutes, or until the exposed crust around the edge of the pizza is golden brown and sounds hollow when you tap it. Repeat with the remaining rounds of dough.

Note: I like to use rectangular baking sheets ❿, but a round one will work, too. Use what you have and, if needed, divide your dough into bigger portions to fit whatever baking sheets you plan to use.

9

10

11

12

BRIOCHE

Makes 1 loaf

INGREDIENTS

500 g all-purpose flour
12 g fresh brewer's yeast
125 g water
4 large eggs
80 g sugar
10 g salt
130 g butter, cut into cubes
Grated zest of 1 orange

1. ❶ Combine the flour, yeast, water, and 3 of the eggs in a bowl and knead for 10 minutes. ❷ Add half of the sugar, knead for 1 minute, and then add the remaining sugar. Add the salt and knead until fairly smooth and homogeneous. Add the chopped butter ❸ and grated orange zest ❹. Knead until unform, about 2 minutes. ❺ The dough should be smooth.

2. Cover and let rest for 6 hours in the refrigerator. ❻

3. The dough should be doubled in size. Line a baking sheet with parchment paper. Divide the dough into three equal parts ❼. Roll each into a log (like a breadstick). Transfer the logs to the prepared baking sheet, setting them side by side. Use your fingers to press one end of each log closed. ❽ Press the three sealed ends together to form the top of your loaf. Next, make the braids ❾ ❿ ⓫ ⓬ by pulling one outside dough piece over the center. Then, cross the opposite side over the new center. Repeat until you reach the end of the dough.

4. Let rise in a warm place for about 2 hours or until puffy and almost doubled in size (see Note).

5. Preheat the oven to 350°F (180°C).

6. In a small bowl, beat the remaining egg. Brush the surface of the braid all over with the egg ⓭ and bake until golden, about 40 minutes.

Note: We're looking for significantly above room temperature, ideally 95°F (35°C). If you own a countertop proofer, this is ideal. If you don't, then look for a warm place in your house such as above the refrigerator (heat rises), near a preheated oven, or simply a sunny spot. If there isn't a warm place in your house, allow more time for the dough to rise.

Microplane

10

11

12

13

CHAPTER 5

HOW TO TASTE A BREAD

MORE THAN JUST A FLAVOR

What is the flavor of a grain? It is a unique combination.

A book dedicated to the great classics of Italian breadmaking that makes you, the affectionate reader, discover those forgotten breads that survive in small places is an ambitious goal. In addition to rediscovering these recipes, describing them allows us to give the proper historical value to each form of bread and to eat them with more attention and awareness. In the same way that when we taste a wine—if we know its history, the area of production, and perhaps the people who produced it, we appreciate it more and value it better—a bread will reveal to us its aromas, its ingredients, and its history.

Instead, we often eat bread without paying attention. Just think about the last time you ate bread—did you even mull over its taste? Almost certainly not (if the answer is yes, well done).

Instead, the last time you had a glass of wine, did you sniff it first? Almost certainly yes. And why doesn't that happen with bread? (I actually do it all the time, and after reading this you will too.)

Here, I think it is important to learn how to taste bread, not just eat it or appreciate it on a cultural level. To fully enjoy it, it is important to understand how to taste it, just as is the case with wine. Each loaf of bread is the result of fermentation, just like a wine or cheese. And then, depending on which flour you used and which processing and baking you chose, you will have different results. How do you distinguish a successful bread from a less successful one? Certainly, visually we have important signs, but then you have to learn to smell it and taste it.

What is the flavor of a grain? It is a unique combination. And what does it come from? From the varieties used and the places where they were grown, that concept that in the wine world the French call *terroir*.

The flavor of a bread derives from the work of the baker, pizza maker, or pastry chef and their choices in processing, fermenting and baking, resulting in flavors being enhanced and new ones developing. In short, the job of the baker is to do justice to the work that the farmer has done in harmony with the land.

To sum up: The farmer, through *terroir* and variety, creates. The miller transforms and has the task of not spoiling the previous work of the farmer but enhancing the flavors and aromas. Bakers, through their labor, close the circle and, if they work well, enhance flavors and create new ones.

I started thinking about how to taste and savor a bread from the early years when I got into the world of leavening, but I did not really have the means to do it. Or rather, we all have the means to savor—and they are the five senses—but I did not know how to use them, and I did not know anyone to ask how to do it. But in life, when you look for something, if you don't lose heart, sooner or later you find it.

And that is how, through a mutual bookseller friend, I met Davide Risso. Who is Davide Risso? He is someone you absolutely must meet if your goal is to understand how taste works. Davide has an interesting background: He is an "anthropologist of taste." He is a molecular biologist who went on to specialize in the molecular science of taste. After his studies, in Pisa and Bologna, he studied for a PhD in taste genetics in the United States and Germany and then completed a postdoctoral fellowship in medical genetics in Seattle. He now works as a leader in a nutrition research group in a large company in London. In short, you get the picture: He is a taste expert.

I met him and we began to exchange a lot of information. I explained to him how we get certain flavors inside a bread and he explained to me how taste works: That, for example, we do not taste with our tongue, but only use it for a small part (some people even think only 5 percent!) and that it is instead the nose (olfactory) that has a preponderant function in perceiving smells. So, I did a test (which I had never done before!): I ate a piece of bread while holding my nose and I realized that it had lost a lot of flavor. Unbelievable. I began to understand that the air that enters our mouth is very important in perceiving smells and, therefore, flavors (so much for those who tell you to eat with your mouth closed!), and that chewing with your mouth open allows you to taste and, therefore, enjoy more. It may not be the best etiquette, but when it comes to tasting a bread, we have to make an exception to the rule.

Even water (saliva) is important for detecting tastes. There are not only four tastes as you have probably been taught (sour, bitter, sweet, and salty), but there is also a fifth called umami, which means "delicious taste" in Japanese. To identify it, think of foods such as meat broth, soy sauce, tomatoes, dried mushrooms, or very aged cheeses such as Parmigiano Reggiano. What do such different foods have in common? They have something salty, even a little sweet, but they are still missing some savory notes that give them a really delicious extra touch: There, that's umami.

That's when I began to get him to explain how it works, and he sketched the diagram below.

This basically means that flavor comes not only from taste but also from smell, temperature, texture, astringency, and chemesthesis.

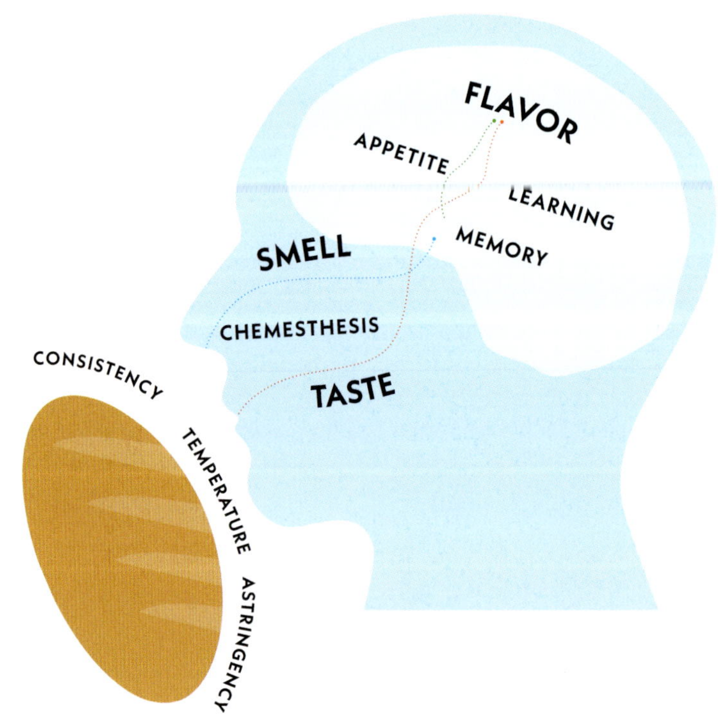

A complicated name, chemesthesis, but it is nothing more than an activation, by chemical compounds we find in foods—such as chile peppers or mint—of temperature receptors that make us sense hot or cold without there being a real change in temperature. And just consider that the famous "map of the tongue" that indicates how tastes can be perceived only in different sections ("bitter" on the bottom, "sour" and "salty" on the sides, "sweet" on the tip) actually does not exist, and all five tastes can be perceived in all its parts.

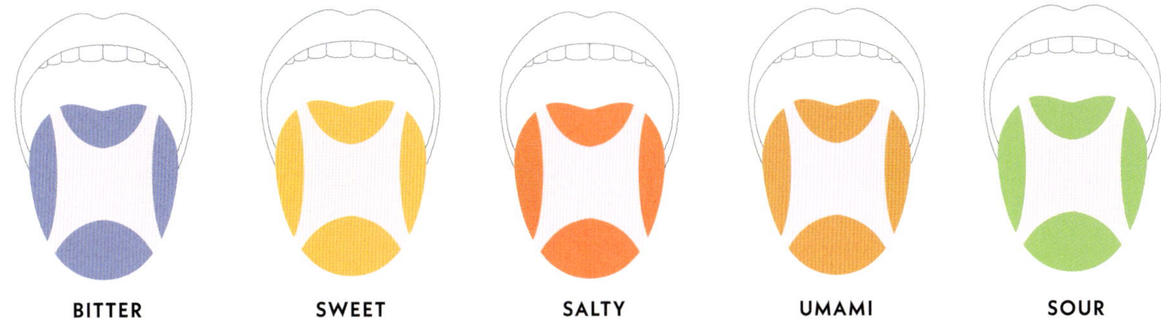

Bakers, through their labor, close the circle and, if they work well, enhance flavors and create new ones.

THE RULES OF TASTING

From my encounters with Davide Risso, we drew up a real tasting map of bread and leavened products, and we came up with some simple rules that I want to share with you here so that the next time you bake a leavened product, or find yourself tasting it, you can actually understand how to savor it.

Maybe you're thinking that the first thing to do to savor a bread is to eat it, but it's actually the last thing you do.

First you look, and what do you look at? The color of the crust, whether it is too white or too dark, which, depending on the bread, should not be raw or even burned. You look at any cuts (patterns) on the crust and assess whether the loaf has "bloomed" well during baking. You see whether there are side splits indicating that the bread has not risen enough or that the flour used is not the right flour, and you check whether there are bubbles on the crust, which often occur when the bread has rested in the refrigerator before being baked.

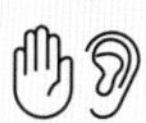

Then you touch it. First you feel whether it is light or heavy and you "knock" the crust, checking that it makes a sound that is not dull, but thumps a little, a sign of good leavening. Then you press the crust lightly to hear the "crunch" and listen for the noise. We squeeze the crumb with our hands or two fingers and check whether it returns back to the initial state. If it remains flattened after squeezing, the bread is not baked enough or there have been problems with leavening.

Then you smell the bread: Squeeze the slice or loaf of bread in your hands and put it in front of your nose, letting air pass through the slice of bread to release the scent. This is a very important stage, when you start to perceive different smells for each loaf of bread, a beautiful world to be discovered and experienced.

Finally, we eat the bread. And we taste it because perhaps it is part of savoring the daily experience that involves the most senses of all. So, we now move on to add the sense of taste, perceiving the five fundamentals (all of them, or a few, depending on the recipe) with every bite.

If we want to properly savor bread, we must separate the crust from the crumb. In the crust, different processes take place in baking than in the crumb. Here then come two separate tastings.

Crumb

Chew the bread many times with your mouth open. (I know, etiquette does not prescribe this, but if you let air into your mouth, it imparts flavors). What notes do you perceive? Sourness? Sweetness? Yogurt? A floury taste? Almond? Grass? Cheese? Green apple? Lemon?

The lactic (cheese) or sour notes (vinegar, lemon) depend on the type of fermentation and the yeast used. The flavor depends, in turn, on the flours and yeast, but also on the fermentation time of the dough. Whole grain flours, for example, give more complex flavors than white flours.

Crust

This is completely different from the crumb. There is the Maillard reaction, which is the caramelization of sugars and proteins during cooking (the process that occurs when cooking a steak). Experience the aromas, tastes, and flavors. Do you taste caramel? Hazelnut? Butter? Roasted wheat? Malt that recalls notes of beer? Do you detect any bitterness? If so, the bread may have been overcooked.

FUOCOFARINA

CHAPTER 6

THE RECIPES

AOSTA VALLEY

MICOULA
CHESTNUT BREAD

Makes 4 loaves

INGREDIENTS

40 g raisins
600 g white whole wheat flour, plus more for dusting
400 g whole grain rye flour
25 g brewer's yeast
500 g warm water
20 g salt
100 g boiled chestnuts (see Note)
100 g dried figs
50 g chopped walnuts
40 g dark chocolate, coarsely chopped

RISE TIME

Rising: 2 hours at room temperature
Proofing: 2 hours at room temperature

BAKE TIME

40 minutes at 400°F (200°C)

1. First, prepare the raisins. Add the raisins to a small bowl and cover with hot water. Set aside.

2. Meanwhile, in a large bowl, combine the whole wheat and rye flours. Add the yeast. Next, and the water a little at a time. Work the mixture together until the dough is smooth and homogeneous, 3 to 5 minutes. Drain the raisins and pat dry with paper towels. Add the raisins, salt, chestnuts, figs, walnuts, and chocolate. Mix until the ingredients are evenly distributed.

3. Cover the dough with plastic wrap and let rise at room temperature for 2 hours.

4. Line a baking sheet with parchment paper. Divide the dough into four equal parts. Shape into even loaves and place them, well spaced, on the prepared baking sheet. Let rise at room temperature for 2 hours.

5. Preheat the oven to 400°F (200°C). Dust the dough generously with whole wheat flour. Score the dough. Bake the dough until the crust is crispy and golden brown, about 40 minutes. Cool and serve.

Note: To boil the chestnuts, first bring a medium pot of water to a boil over high heat. Rinse the chestnuts and score each, taking care to cut through the shell but not the nutmeat inside. Add the whole chestnuts to the boiling water. Cook until the inside meat is tender, about 20 minutes. Drain, cool, and peel.

Did you know...

Micoula boasts medieval origins. It used to be a simple chestnut bread associated with the Aosta Valley but was later enriched with dried fruits and other ingredients, becoming a specialty at end-of-year festivities. In patois—an Aosta Valley variant of the Provençal language—its name literally means "smaller, special bread." It keeps for a long time when tightly sealed in a paper bag and is excellent served with jam or even paired with cheeses.

AOSTA VALLEY

TEGOLE VALDOSTANE

ALMOND HAZELNUT COOKIES

Makes about 2 dozen cookies

INGREDIENTS

80 g shelled almonds (see Note)
80 g shelled hazelnuts (see Note)
200 g sugar
160 g egg whites (from about 5 large eggs)
Pinch of salt
60 g butter, melted
60 g all-purpose flour
Pinch of vanilla seeds

BAKE TIME

10 to 12 minutes at 350°F (180°C)

1. Preheat the oven to 350°F (180°C).

2. Add the almonds and hazelnuts to a rimmed sheet pan. Spread into an even layer and bake for about 10 minutes. Allow the nuts to cool for 5 to 10 minutes.

3. Transfer to a blender or food processor. Add the sugar and process on high speed until smooth, about 5 minutes. Transfer to a large bowl and set aside.

4. Using a stand mixer or electric mixer set to medium speed, whip the egg whites and salt for 2 minutes. Increase the speed to high and whip until stiff peaks form, about 3 more minutes.

5. Add the melted butter, flour, and vanilla seeds to the nut mixture. Stir until incorporated. Spoon the egg whites on top and then gently incorporate, stirring with a spatula from the bottom up so the eggs don't lose their fluffy texture.

6. Line a baking sheet with parchment paper. Spoon small mounds of the mixture onto the prepared sheet, about 2 inches (5 cm) apart. Use the spoon, your hands, or a cookie cutter to shape the mounds into flat rounds. Bake for 10 to 12 minutes, or until golden brown along the edges but lightly golden in the center. Allow them to cool completely on a wire rack before serving.

7. The cookies will keep for 3 to 4 days if stored in an airtight container.

Note: For an extra special touch, add a pinch of cinnamon when you roast the nuts. Another way to add even more flavor is to add grated lemon zest to the dough.

Did you know...

The curious name of these cookies comes from the habit of drying them on a rolling pin, which gives them their typical convex shape like roof tiles (*tegole*).

AOSTA VALLEY

FLANDZE

SWEET RAISIN BUNS

Makes 12 to 15 buns

INGREDIENTS

500 g pastry or cake flour
100 g sugar, plus 50 g sugar for dusting
12 g fresh brewer's yeast
4 large eggs
150 g whole milk
10 g salt
125 g butter, cubed
50 g raisins
50 g pine nuts
1 large egg white, beaten

RISE TIME

Rising: 1 hour
Proofing: 2 hours

BAKE TIME

30 minutes at 350°F (180°C)

1. In a large bowl, mix the flour, 100 g of the sugar, yeast, eggs, and 130 g of the milk until a smooth dough forms, 3 to 5 minutes. Add the remaining 20 g of whole milk and the salt and mix for 10 minutes. The dough should be elastic. Cut in the butter. Lastly, add the raisins and pine nuts and mix until evenly distributed.

2. Lightly dampen a tea towel with water. Cover the bowl with the tea towel and let rise for 1 hour at room temperature.

3. Line a baking sheet with parchment paper. Shape the dough into balls (about the size of a golf ball), place them on the prepared baking sheet, and brush them with the egg white. Allow to rise at room temperature for 2 more hours.

4. Preheat the oven to 350°F (180°C).

5. Score the surface of the buns with a knife, sprinkle evenly with the remaining 50 g of sugar, and bake until golden brown, about 30 minutes.

Did you know...

Flandze (or *flantze*) is a sweet flatbread flavored with dried fruit. It has a soft texture, typical of Valdostan tradition. Its round shape is said to symbolize the sun while the process of browning (baking it) is said to symbolize the rebirth of nature. Very versatile, it can be enjoyed at any time of the day. Enjoy it for breakfast or as an after-meal dessert.

BIOVA
PIEDMONTESE SOURDOUGH BREAD

Makes 3 or 4 loaves

INGREDIENTS

For the *biga* (starter)

5 g brewer's yeast
250 g warm water
500 g pastry or cake flour

For the dough

500 g all-purpose flour
350 g water
5 g diastatic malt powder (see Note)
22 g salt

RISE TIME

First rise: 18 hours
Proofing: 1 hour

BAKE TIME

25 minutes at 450°F (230°C)

1. Make the *biga*: In a large bowl, whisk together the yeast and water until the yeast is fully dissolved. Add the pastry flour and mix. Do not knead. Cover with plastic wrap and let rise for 18 hours. A cool spot, about 68°F (20°C), is best, but room temperature will suffice.

2. Next, make the dough: In a large bowl, work together the *biga* with the all-purpose flour, water, malt powder, and salt. Once a smooth dough forms, cover and let rest for 30 minutes.

3. Divide the dough into 3 or 4 portions, about 453 g (1 cup) each. One by one, turn out the dough balls on a floured work surface and shape into loaves. Let rest for 10 minutes. Flatten each with a rolling pin so that they look like long, narrow "tongues" that you are going to roll from the long side, giving them the shape of a snail. Let rise for 50 minutes.

4. Preheat the oven to 450°F (230°C).

5. Use a sharp blade to split each loaf down the middle. Arrange cut side up on a baking sheet and bake until the crust is deep golden brown, about 25 minutes.

Note: Diastatic malt powder can be purchased online.

Did you know...

Of ancient origin, *biova* is an oblong-shaped Piedmontese bread. The crust is crisp and is marked by a split down the center. The size varies and the name even changes according to the bread's weight! Larger loaves are called *biovona* while smaller loaves are called *biovetta*.

PIEDMONT

PIZZA AL PADELLINO

SKILLET PIZZA

Makes 3 pizzas

INGREDIENTS

For the dough

1 kg all-purpose flour, plus more for dusting

600 g warm water

12 g fresh brewer's yeast

40 g extra virgin olive oil

25 g salt

Optional toppings

Tomato puree

Sliced mushrooms

Sliced artichoke hearts

Prosciutto cotto or prosciutto

Sliced olives

Extra virgin olive oil

RISE TIME

First rise: 1 hour

Second rise: 30 minutes

Proofing: 1 hour

BAKE TIME

20 minutes at 475°F (240°C)

1. In a large bowl, mix together the flour, water, yeast, oil, and half of the salt. Using your hands, work the mixture until a smooth dough forms. This should take about 10 minutes. Transfer the dough to a greased bowl, cover, and let rise for 1 hour.

2. Divide the dough into three pieces (each should be just over 500 g [1 lb]). Dust your hands with flour and form the dough into balls.

3. Grease three round 9-inch (23 cm) pizza pans (a pizza stone will work, as well). Place one dough ball in the center of each prepared pan. Let rise for 30 minutes.

4. Next, dust a clean surface with flour. Roll out each dough until it is 9 inches (23 cm) in diameter. Transfer each dough back to its respective pizza pan. Divide the tomato puree evenly among the three pizza crusts. Brush the puree out until each crust is evenly covered. Let rise for 1 hour at room temperature.

5. Preheat the oven to 475°F (240°C). Bake each pizza until the dough is cooked through and the outer crust is crispy, about 20 minutes. Top the pizza with the rest of the ingredients, or with whatever toppings you would like, and serve.

Did you know...

In Turin, Italy, this pizza is known for its tall, thick dough that is baked in the oven inside a small round aluminum (or iron) pan without handles, called a *padellino* or *tegamino*. Soft on the inside and crispy on the outside, this pizza dough works well with all kinds of toppings, as seen in this recipe.

PIEDMONT

TIRÀ

SWEET RAISIN BREAD

Makes 1 loaf

INGREDIENTS

1 kg all-purpose flour
20 g fresh brewer's yeast
140 g extra-fine sugar
75 g solid sourdough starter (optional, see page 76)
300 g warm water
5 large eggs
20 g salt
250 g butter, cubed
150 g raisins
300 g sugared apples, diced (see Note)
Pearl sugar, or other sugar, for dusting

RISE TIME

First rise: 40 minutes
Second rise: 50 minutes
Proofing: 90 minutes

BAKE TIME

45 minutes at 350°F (180°C)

1. Combine the flour, brewer's yeast, extra-fine sugar, and sourdough starter (if using) in a large bowl or the bowl of a stand mixer fitted with a dough hook. Add the water and mix on low speed, or stir by hand. Add the eggs one at a time. Mix on low for 20 to 30 minutes. The dough should be smooth, elastic, and slightly sticky.

2. With the mixer set to low, add the salt. Next, add the butter a little at a time. Finally, add the raisins, and mix until evenly distributed.

3. Transfer the dough to a greased bowl, cover with plastic wrap, and let rise for 40 minutes.

4. Fold the dough in on itself, keeping it inside the bowl at all times. Cover and let rise for another 50 minutes.

5. Turn the dough out onto a clean work surface. Use your hands to spread the dough into a rectangle. Spread the diced apples in the center and roll the dough from the long side, shaping it like a stuffed sausage.

6. Line a baking sheet with parchment paper. Transfer the dough to the prepared pan and let it rise until doubled in volume, about 1½ hours.

7. Preheat the oven to 350°F (180°C). Sprinkle the dough with pearl sugar and bake until dark brown (but not burned!), about 45 minutes.

Note: The original Italian recipe calls for candied apples. If you happen to have those, toss them in! If not, simply peel and dice apples and sauté them in a pan with sugar. Cook until just tender, 5 to 10 minutes.

Did you know...

The *tirà* is a sweet bread topped with raisins that originated in Rocchetta Tanaro, in the Monferrato area of Asti. The name appears to be related to the festivals (*al tiráj*) during which young men called to arms went to pull a number (*tirare il numero*). Another theory for the name is that it derives from the method of making it, which involves stretching and pulling (*tirare*) the dough before forming a sausage shape.

PANE DI TRIORA

TRIORA WHITE BREAD

Makes 4 loaves

INGREDIENTS

1 kg high-gluten flour
6 g fresh brewer's yeast
650 g water
20 g salt
Wheat bran, for dusting

RISE TIME

First rise: 2 hours
Proofing: 3 hours

BAKE TIME

40 minutes at 400°F (200°C)

1. In a large bowl, mix the flour, yeast, and 600 g of the water. Let rest for 5 minutes. Add the salt and the remaining 50 g of water and knead until the dough is smooth and homogeneous, about 10 minutes.

2. Place the dough in a large bowl, cover with plastic wrap, and let rise at room temperature for 2 hours. Your dough should be roughly doubled in size.

3. Dust a baking dish generously with wheat bran. Divide the dough in half. Form two round loaves and place them in the prepared baking dish. Let rise for 3 hours at room temperature. The dough should be puffy.

4. Preheat the oven to 400°F (200°C). Bake until golden, fluffy, and cooked through, 40 minutes.

Did you know...

This homemade bread is a typical product of Triora, Italy, a medieval village located in the Valle Argentina, in the province of Imperia, known as "the village of witches." It is typically baked on wooden boards sprinkled with bran, which serve to prevent the dough from sticking. The golden crust hides a beige crumb with fine, regular dimpling; its shelf life is excellent.

LIGURIA

FOCACCIA LIGURE

LIGURIAN FOCACCIA

Makes 4 (12 x 16-inch [30 x 41 cm]) focaccia

INGREDIENTS

For the dough

1 kg all-purpose flour, plus more for dusting

10 g fresh brewer's yeast

580 g warm water

22 g salt

80 g extra virgin olive oil

For the brine

400 g water

30 g salt

200 g extra virgin olive oil

RISE TIME

First rise: 1 hour

Second rise: 1 hour

Proofing: 45 minutes

BAKE TIME

20 minutes at 475°F (240°C)

1. Make the dough: In a large bowl, mix the flour, yeast, and water until evenly combined. Add the salt and oil, a little at a time, then knead until you have a smooth, soft, shaggy dough. Transfer the dough to an oiled bowl, cover with plastic wrap, and let rise for 1 hour.

2. Turn the dough out onto a floured work surface and divide it into four equal portions (about 600 g each). Generously grease four 12- by 16-inch (30 by 41 cm) baking sheets. Let rise, uncovered, for 1 hour.

3. Stretch each dough to the edges of its pan, taking care to ensure the dough is distributed evenly. If it shrinks, wait 30 minutes and stretch it again. Let the dough rest at room temperature for 45 minutes.

4. Make the brine: In a medium bowl, mix together the water, salt, and olive oil. Dip your fingers into the brine and then, using a fair amount of pressure, press down into the dough to make dimples. Rewet your hands with the brine and repeat until all of the dough is evenly dimpled. Let stand for 10 minutes.

5. Preheat the oven to 475°F (240°C) and bake until golden brown, about 20 minutes.

Did you know...

Genoese focaccia—or *fugassa* as it is known in the region—is one of the culinary symbols of Liguria, but is loved well beyond the region. Soft and flavorful, it is distinguished by its long leavening and characteristic holes, which are flavored with brine. This bread was once the classic mid-morning meal of the longshoremen. Today, it is eaten at any time of the day, starting with breakfast, when it can be dunked in a cappuccino.

PANDOLCE GENOVESE

SWEET GENOESE FRUIT BREAD

Makes 1 large round bread

INGREDIENTS

For refreshing the sourdough starter

150 g all-purpose flour
100 g sourdough starter (see page 76)
75 g water

For the dough

250 g all-purpose flour
180 g sugar
15 g honey
125 g whole milk
16 g salt
150 g butter
Grated zest of 1 orange
175 g raisins, soaked in water until plump
60 g pine nuts
120 g candied fruit, diced
1 large egg, beaten

RISE TIME

Leavening: 4 hours
First rise: 1 hour
Proofing: 6 hours

BAKE TIME

50 minutes at 325°F (160°C)

1. Refresh the sourdough starter: In a large bowl, mix together the flour, sourdough starter, and water. Cover with plastic wrap and let rest in a warm area for 4 hours (see Note).

2. Make the dough: In a large bowl, work the sourdough together with the flour, sugar, honey, milk and salt. Next, add the butter and grated orange zest and mix until absorbed. Strain the raisins and add them to the dough, along with the pine nuts and diced candied fruit, evenly distributing them. Let rise for 1 hour at room temperature.

3. Divide the dough into two parts, forming balls. Place in a baking dish, cover with plastic wrap, and let rise for about 6 hours.

4. Brush the surface of the *pandolce* with the beaten egg and score it by making three cuts forming a triangle.

5. Preheat the oven to 325°F (160°C) and bake for 50 minutes, until golden brown. Remove from the oven and let cool.

Note: The ideal temperature for this rise is at 86°F (30°C). Commercial bakers have the advantage of bread proofers that can be set to specific temperatures. Home cooks don't have that advantage, but many of us have houses with warm areas. Seek out a warmer area in your house such as a windowsill, above your refrigerator, or anywhere else you can think of.

Did you know...

Pandolce Genovese boasts a very ancient history. In fact, it seems to derive from the sweet breads enriched with fruit and honey that the Egyptians and Greeks offered in homage to the deities. According to one legend, it was the Genoese admiral and statesman Andrea Doria who, in the 16th century, asked local pastry chefs to create a dessert that would both exalt the republic and keep well during long sea voyages.

MICHETTA
MILANESE ROUND LOAF

Makes 8 medium rolls

INGREDIENTS

For the *biga* (starter)
900 g cake flour
9 g fresh brewer's yeast
450 g warm water

For the dough
100 g all-purpose flour
5 g diastatic malt powder
50 g water
22 g salt
Extra virgin olive oil, for brushing

RISE TIME
First rise: 18 hours
Second rise: 30 minutes
Third rise: 50 minutes
Fourth rise: 45 minutes

BAKING
20 minutes at 450°F (230°C)

1. Make the *biga*: In a large bowl, combine the cake flour, yeast, and warm water. Knead until a shaggy dough forms. Cover with a tea towel or plastic wrap, set in a cool place (see Note), and let rise for 18 hours.

2. Make the dough: Add the flour, malt powder, and water to the *biga*. Once combined, add the salt and knead 1 to 2 minutes more. Cover and let rest for about 30 minutes.

3. Form a ball with the dough, roll it out with a rolling pin, then roll it on itself and form it into a round shape. Brush the surface with extra virgin oil and let it rise for 50 minutes. Roll out the dough to a thickness of 1¼ inches (3 cm) and cut out circular disks with a 4-inch (10 cm) biscuit cutter or round cookie cutter. Use a specialty *michetta* bread cutter or an apple cutter to press lines into the disks. Turn them over and let them rise for 45 minutes at room temperature.

4. Bring a medium, ovenproof pot of water to a boil over medium-high heat. Meanwhile, preheat the oven to 450°F (230°C) with one rack in the lowest position and one in the middle. Add the pot to the lowest rack of the oven.

5. Flip the rolls over again, so that the design is facing up, and bake until golden, about 20 minutes. The pot of water should create steam, which is necessary for a proper bake of this bread.

Note: For rising, we're aiming for 65°F to 68°F (18°C to 20°C), so places that stay cool are best. Try a pantry or basement.

Did you know...

The *michetta* is a typically Milanese round loaf that is widespread throughout the Lombardy region. It belongs to the family of "puffed" breads, that is, hollow on the inside, and is characterized by five overlying cuts, which are made with special molds.

BRUSADELA ROMAGNESE

CRUNCHY ROMAGNESE FOCACCIA

Makes 4 medium rounds

INGREDIENTS

500 g white whole wheat flour
500 g all-purpose flour
600 g water
12 g fresh brewer's yeast
22 g salt
50 g extra virgin olive oil, plus more as needed

RISE TIME

First rise: 2 hours
Proofing: 40 minutes at room temperature

BAKE TIME

20 to 25 minutes at 475°F (240°C)

1. In a large bowl, mix the white whole wheat and all-purpose flours, water, and yeast for 10 minutes. Add the salt and mix until absorbed. Add the oil and mix until thoroughly incorporated. Knead until smooth. Cover and let rise at room temperature for 2 hours.

2. Generously oil a large baking dish (see Note). Divide the dough into four equal pieces and shape them into rounds. Place them in the prepared pan and let them rise for about 40 minutes.

3. Meanwhile, preheat the oven as high as it will go without setting it to broil. For most ovens, that's about 500°F (260°C).

4. With oiled hands, gently roll out the balls until they are about ¾ inch (2 cm) high. Bake each for 20 to 25 minutes, until some of the airy bubbles are slightly burned and the focaccia is light, airy, golden all over, and cooked through. You may need to work in batches.

Note: It's important to check the heat rating on your baking dish. Not all baking dishes can withstand temperatures of 500°F (260°C), so pick your dish carefully and take care to avoid sudden changes in temperature (setting a hot dish on a cold counter, for example).

Did you know...

Round and crispy, the *brusadela* was made by accident: In Romagnese, in Oltrepò Pavese, it was in fact customary to test the oven temperature with a piece of dough before baking bread. The result of the test was an excellent but slightly burned *focaccina*, the very characteristic from which the bread derives its name. Traditionally, *brusadela* is baked on refractory stone, which gives it a special crunchiness. There is also a sweet version. And, in the town where it was invented, there's even a festival each year dedicated to this.

FUOCOFARINA

TORTA DELLE ROSE

ROSE PASTRY

Makes 8 medium rolls

INGREDIENTS

For the dough

1 kg all-purpose flour

25 g fresh brewer's yeast (or 1⅓ cups refreshed sourdough)

200 g water

200 g whole milk

150 g sugar

4 large eggs

50 g honey (acacia honey, if possible)

12 g salt

200 g butter, softened

For the filling

200 g butter

10 g ground cinnamon

RISE TIME

First rise: Overnight

Second rise: 1 hour

Third rise: 2 hours

Proofing: 2 hours

BAKE TIME

30 minutes at 350°F (180°C)

1. Make the dough: In a large bowl, mix the flour, water, milk, sugar, eggs, and honey for about 10 minutes. Add the salt and incorporate the butter. Let the dough rest overnight in a bowl covered with plastic wrap.

2. The next day, roll out the dough with a rolling pin to a thickness of about ¼ inch (6 mm).

3. Make the filling: Coat the dough with the butter and a sprinkling of cinnamon. Roll into a spiral starting from the longest side, without pressing too tightly, then place in the refrigerator for 1 hour.

4. Cut the roll into slices about 2 inches (5 cm) thick, then arrange them spiral-side up in a buttered baking dish. Let rise for 2 more hours in a warm place (82°F [28°C] is ideal, but not required).

5. Preheat the oven to 350°F (180°C) and bake the pastry until golden, about 30 minutes. Remove from the oven and let cool.

Did you know...

Among the most traditional delights of the Mantuan tradition, this leavened pastry is prepared by slicing a roll of dough coated with creamed butter into rounds. The slices, arranged in a circle to cover the entire surface of the cake pan, rise to form a single body that looks like a bouquet of roses. As for its origins, the pastry is said to have been created to pay homage to the noblewoman Isabella d'Este and prepared for her wedding banquet with Francesco II Gonzaga, marquis of Mantua, in 1490.

TRENTINO-ALTO ADIGE

PAARL

SOURDOUGH RYE BREAD

Makes 8 small breads

INGREDIENTS

1 kg whole meal rye flour, plus more for dusting

650 g warm water (about 100°F [38°C])

22 g salt

200 g liquid cultured yeast (see page 77)

RISE TIME

First rise: 1 hour

Proofing: 2 hours

BAKE TIME

25 minutes at 475°F (240°C)

1. Add the rye flour to the bowl of a stand mixer fitted with a paddle attachment. Add the warm water and mix. Add the salt and sourdough, mix again, and let everything rest in the bowl of the mixer for about 1 hour.

2. Sprinkle a work surface with rye flour. Turn the dough out onto the work surface and shape into 8 balls that are about 8 ounces (227 g) each.

3. Line a baking sheet with parchment paper. Arrange the balls on the prepared baking sheet so that pairs of dough balls are close enough together to slightly touch (see "Did you know..." below). Let them rise for 2 hours at room temperature. When the rise is complete, using a sieve, dust the loaves with rye flour.

4. Preheat the oven to 475°F (240°C) and bake, with plenty of steam (see Note), for about 25 minutes.

Note: To make steam in your oven, bring a medium, ovenproof pot of water to a boil over medium-high heat. Meanwhile, preheat the oven with one rack in the lowest position and one in the middle. Add the pot to the lowest rack of the oven and your *paarl* to the middle rack.

Did you know...

A Val Venosta tradition, this bread is characterized by its dark color and intense flavor, imparted by whole grain rye flour. The shape is also peculiar and is made by joining two round, flat loaves of bread: The name, in fact, means "pair." It is excellent with savory foods, especially speck, or desserts, such as delicious local apricot jam.

TRENTINO-ALTO ADIGE

SCHÜTTELBROT

RUSTIC TYROLEAN RYE BREAD

Makes 8 to 10 small flatbreads

INGREDIENTS

For the pre-dough

300 g rye flour

10 g fresh brewer's yeast, crumbled

300 g warm water (86°F [30°C])

For the dough

600 g rye flour

300 g all-purpose flour, plus more for dusting

1 L warm water (86°F [30°C])

20 g salt

10 g fennel seeds

10 g ground cumin or cumin seeds

RISE TIME

First rise: 1 hour

Proofing: 2 hours

BAKE TIME

30 minutes at 425°F (220°C)

1. Make the pre-dough: In a large bowl, mix the rye flour, crumbled yeast, and warm water (86°F [30°C]) and mix until smooth and soft. Cover the bowl with a damp tea towel and let rise in a warm place for about 1 hour.

2. Make the dough: Add the rye flour, all-purpose flour, warm water, salt, fennel seeds, and cumin (or mixed seeds to taste) to the risen pre-dough. Mix everything together for 10 minutes until the dough is well blended and as firm as possible. If needed, add a little water or flour.

3. Cover the dough with a damp tea towel and let it rise in a warm place for 2 hours. When doubled in volume, divide the dough into eight or ten equal portions and arrange them on a floured work surface. Shape each into a smooth ball, then cover with a dampened cloth and let rest for 15 minutes.

4. Take each ball and roll it vigorously back and forth with your hands on the lightly floured work surface, pressing it with your palms until you get a disk about ⅒ inch (3 mm) thick. Line a baking sheet with parchment paper.

5. Preheat the oven to 425°F (220°C) (218°C). Place the disks on the prepared baking sheet and bake for 30 minutes or until golden brown. It's okay if the disks touch.

6. Once baked, let the disks cool slightly on a wire rack. Then, gently, using your fingers or the back of a knife, break them apart into small, crispy, crumbly breads.

Did you know...

This crusty rye bread is a Tyrolean specialty with a rustic flavor, enriched with fennel and cumin. The name "shaken bread," a literal translation of *Schüttelbrot*, originates from the traditional method of making it: The loaves have to be beaten and flattened by hand on a wooden board and, as a result of this process, they become hard and crumbly after baking.

TRENTINO-ALTO ADIGE

BRAZADEL

SUGAR BREAD

Makes 1 (10-inch [26 cm]) brazadel or 26 small brazadel

INGREDIENTS

For the dough

1 kg pastry or cake flour, plus more for dusting

15 g fresh brewer's yeast

250 g whole milk

7 large eggs

180 g granulated sugar

18 g salt

200 g butter, cubed, slightly softened

For brushing and topping

1 large egg, beaten

Pearl sugar or other large-granule sugar

Grated zest of 1 lemon, optional

RISE TIME

First rise: 2 hours

Proofing: 1 hour

BAKE TIME

30 to 35 minutes at 350°F (180°C)

1. Make the dough: In a large bowl, mix together the flour, yeast, milk, and eggs. Mix for 10 minutes. Add half the granulated sugar, stir, and then add the remaining sugar. Mix until incorporated. Add the salt and mix vigorously for about 10 minutes, until a smooth, homogeneous mass is obtained.

2. Incorporate the butter, a little at a time, continuing to mix until it is completely absorbed.

3. Cover the bowl with a damp tea towel and let rise in a warm place for about 2 hours, or until doubled in volume.

4. Turn the risen dough out onto a floured work surface and knead it until deflated, 1 to 2 minutes. Form a hole in the center and shape the mixture into a ring-shaped cake (see Note). Line a tube pan with parchment paper. Gently arrange the dough in the prepared pan. Cover with a dampened tea towel and let rise until doubled in size, about 1 hour.

5. Make the topping: Brush the surface all over with beaten egg and sprinkle with the pearl sugar and optional lemon zest.

6. Preheat the oven to 350°F (180°C) and bake for 30 to 35 minutes, until golden brown. Remove from the oven and let it cool completely on a wire rack before eating it.

Note: You can use a donut pan to make personal-size breads, if you prefer.

Did you know...

Also known as *brazedèl* or *brazadè*, this is a soft-textured Trentino *ciambella* associated with the end-of-year festivities. The origins seem to date back to the Middle Ages, and the name comes from the fact that it was carried as a gift on New Year's Eve, as a sign of good luck, tucked under the arm (*braccio*). The recipe calls for simple ingredients such as flour, yeast, butter, sugar, and milk; depending on the area and family traditions, other ingredients may be added, including raisins, pine nuts, lemon peel, and grappa.

VENETO

CIABATTA

Makes 4 medium breads

INGREDIENTS

For the *biga* (starter)

9 g fresh brewer's yeast
450 g water
900 g bread flour

For the dough

100 g bread flour, plus more for dusting
350 g water
10 g diastatic malt powder
22 g salt

LEAVENING

First rise: 16 to 18 hours
Second rise: 2 hours
Third rise: 2 hours

BAKING

15 to 18 minutes at 450°F (230°C)

1. Make the *biga*: In a large bowl, dissolve the yeast in the water, add the flour, and knead with your hands until combined, but not smooth. Cover with plastic wrap and let rest for 16 to 18 hours at a maximum temperature of 68°F (20°C).

2. Make the dough: Once the *biga* has fermented, add the flour, half the water, and malt and begin kneading. Incorporate the salt and, gradually add the remaining water, continuing to knead the dough until it is smooth and even. Place it in a large mixing bowl, cover with plastic wrap, and let it rest at room temperature until doubled in volume, about 2 hours.

3. Roll the dough out on a well-floured work surface and divide it into 4 rectangles, making them as even as possible. Transfer to a floured dish towel and let rise for 2 hours at room temperature.

4. Preheat the oven to 450°F (230°C). Transfer the ciabatta to a baking sheet lined with baking paper or to a well-heated oven stone, arranging them upside down, and bake for 15 to 18 minutes with plenty of steam (see Note). You're looking for a light, airy bread with a golden top.

Note: To make steam in your oven, bring a medium, ovenproof pot of water to a boil over medium-high heat. Meanwhile, preheat the oven with one rack in the lowest position and one in the middle. Add the pot to the lowest rack of the oven and your ciabatta to the middle rack.

Did you know...

The ciabatta is a bread with an elongated, flattened shape, a golden, crispy outer crust etched with longitudinal cuts, and a well-veined crumb. Its origins are from the Veneto region. It was invented by Arnaldo Cavallari, a former rally champion who later decided to devote himself to the family mill in Adria, Polesine. In September 1982, Cavallari registered this type of bread—now widespread throughout Italy—with the name Ciabatta Italia.

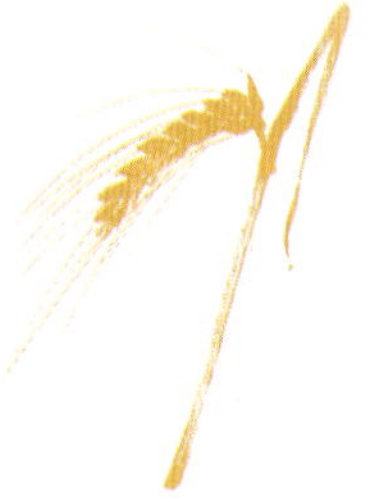

FUOCOFARINA

SCHISSOTTO PADOVANO

PADUAN FOCACCIA

Makes 1 Paduan focaccia

INGREDIENTS

500 g bread flour, plus more for dusting
6 g fresh brewer's yeast
250 g water
20 g sugar
10 g salt
40 g extra virgin olive oil
20 g grappa, preferably, or apple brandy or pear brandy
80 g lard, melted (optional)

RISE TIME

First rise: 2 hours
Proofing: 1 hour

BAKE TIME

40 to 50 minutes at 400°F (200°C)

1. In a large bowl, combine the flour, yeast, water, sugar, salt, oil, and grappa. Mix vigorously for about 10 minutes, until a smooth, homogeneous mass is obtained. If it is too soft, add 1 tablespoon (8 g) of flour at a time until the desired consistency is reached.
2. Cover the bowl with a damp tea towel and let rise in a warm place for about 2 hours or until doubled in volume.
3. Transfer the dough to a floured surface and knead it briefly until deflated, then shape it into a rectangle and make diamond-shaped incisions on the surface.
4. Place it in a baking pan lined with parchment paper, cover it with a damp cloth, and let it rise again for about 1 hour. After this time, if you like, brush the surface of the *schissotto* with melted lard.
5. Preheat the oven to 400°F (200°C) and bake for 40 to 50 minutes, until golden brown. Remove from the oven and let it cool completely on a wire rack.

Did you know...

Also known as *Colli Euganei* or *Montagnana* bread, this is a rustic and flavorful focaccia bread native to the rural areas of Padua. Its name derives from the Venetian verb *schissare*, meaning "to crunch," in reference to its crispy crust that tends to crunch during chewing. The original recipe did not call for yeast.

FOCACCIA VENETA

SWEET VENETIAN FOCACCIA

Makes 2 loaves

INGREDIENTS

For the first dough

250 g bread flour
250 g all-purpose flour
12 g fresh brewer's yeast
300 g whole milk
20 g granulated sugar

For the second dough

500 g bread flour, plus more for dusting
300 g granulated sugar
5 large eggs
150 g butter, at room temperature
1 vanilla bean, seeds only
Grated zest of 1 lemon
8 g salt
1 egg white, beaten
Pearl sugar or large-granule sugar, for sprinkling

RISE TIME

First rise: 1 hour
Second rise: 2 hours
Proofing: 2 hours

BAKE TIME

40 to 50 minutes at 350°F (180°C)

1. Make the first dough: In a large bowl, mix together the bread and all-purpose flours with the yeast. Add the milk and granulated sugar and mix until the dough is smooth and sticky. Cover the bowl with a damp tea towel and let rise in a warm place for about 1 hour, until doubled in size.

2. Make the second dough: In a large bowl, combine the first risen dough with the bread flour, granulated sugar, eggs, butter, vanilla seeds, grated lemon peel, and salt.

3. Mix vigorously for about 10 minutes, until the mass is smooth and uniform. If it is too soft, add a tablespoon of flour at a time until the desired consistency is reached.

4. Cover the bowl with a damp tea towel and let rise in a warm place for about 2 hours.

5. Turn the dough out onto a floured pastry board and divide it in half. Form two 24-inch (61 cm) long loaves, twist each into a ring, and place them on a baking sheet lined with parchment paper. Brush the surface with the beaten egg white and let rise for another 2 hours at room temperature.

6. Preheat the oven to 350°F (180°C). Brush the buns again with the egg white and sprinkle with pearl sugar, then bake for 40 to 50 minutes, or until golden brown. Remove from the oven and allow to cool completely.

Did you know...

Also known as *fugassa*, this is a leavened cake typical of the Easter holidays, whose ringed shape symbolizes rebirth. Its soft texture and rich, wholesome flavor make it perfect at any time of year to accompany coffee or tea, for breakfast, and for snacks.

FRIULI-VENEZIA GIULIA

BIGA SERVOLANA

WHITE SERVOLANA BUNS

Makes 12 medium buns

INGREDIENTS

For the *biga* (starter)

700 g pastry or cake flour

350 g warm water (about 100°F [38°C])

10 g brewer's yeast

For the dough

300 g all-purpose flour

250 g warm water (about 100°F [38°C])

5 g diastatic malt powder

22 g salt

50 g lard

RISE TIME

First rise: 12 to 18 hours

Second rise: 6 to 8 hours

Proofing: 2 hours

BAKE TIME

40 to 50 minutes at 400°F (200°C)

1. Make the *biga*: In a large bowl, mix the pastry flour with the water and the yeast; mix briefly until smooth and sticky, then cover with a damp tea towel and let rise in a warm place for 12 to 18 hours, until doubled in volume.
2. Make the dough: Combine the all-purpose flour, *biga*, warm water, malt, salt, and lard in another large bowl.
3. Work everything vigorously for about 10 minutes so that the dough is smooth and homogeneous, then cover the bowl with a damp cloth and let rise in a warm place for 6 to 8 hours, until doubled in size.
4. Divide dough into 12 3- to 3½-ounce (80 to 100 g) pieces. Make smooth, round balls and pair them two by two, so that each pair makes a shape like the number 8.
5. Place them on a baking sheet lined with parchment paper, cover with a dampened cloth, and let rise again for about 2 hours, or until doubled in volume. Using a small knife, score the center.
6. Preheat the oven to 400°F (200°C) and bake the buns for 40 to 50 minutes, until golden brown.
7. Remove the buns from the oven and allow them to cool completely on a wire rack before serving.

Did you know...

Biga servolana is a typical bread from Trieste, whose origins date back to the 16th century. Its main characteristic is its long rising time. It was prepared by the skilled hands of the women of Servola, a district of Trieste, who handed down the recipe from generation to generation. Even today this bread is a symbol of the local culinary tradition and is produced by a few artisan bakeries.

FRIULI-VENEZIA GIULIA

PAN DE SORC

SWEET FRIULIAN CORNBREAD

Makes 4 medium-small breads

INGREDIENTS

For the polenta

600 g water

300 g Cinquantino corn flour or wholemeal yellow corn flour

For the dough

600 g white whole wheat flour

100 g white rye flour

250 g solid sourdough starter (see page 76) or 3½ teaspoons [10 g] fresh brewer's yeast

450 g water

100 g raisins

50 g dried figs, chopped

10 fennel seeds

2 g ground cinnamon

20 g salt

Cornmeal, for dusting

RISE TIME

First rise: 1 hour

Proofing: 2 hours 30 minutes

BAKE TIME

25 minutes at 400°F (200°C)

1. Make the polenta: Bring the water to a boil in a saucepan, then sprinkle in the flour. Cook, stirring frequently with a whisk to prevent lumps from forming, until the polenta has thickened enough to make it difficult to continue whisking. Set aside and allow to cool.
2. Make the dough: In a large bowl, mix the wheat and rye flours together, add the sourdough and water, and mix until the dough is smooth. Add the now cooled polenta and gently fold in the raisins, chopped figs, fennel seeds, cinnamon, and salt.
3. Let rise in the bowl covered with plastic wrap for about 1 hour, then divide the dough into 4 balls.
4. Dust them with cornmeal, make a crosscut in the surface with a knife, place them on a baking sheet lined with parchment paper, and cover them with a freshly dampened tea towel. Let them rise for 2 hours and 30 minutes.
5. Preheat the oven to 400°F (200°C) and bake, with plenty of steam (see Note), for about 25 minutes or until golden.

Note: To make steam in your oven, bring a medium, ovenproof pot of water to a boil over medium-high heat. Meanwhile, preheat the oven with one rack in the lowest position and one in the middle. Add the pot to the lowest rack of the oven and your bread to the middle rack.

Did you know...

Pan de sorc is a sweet, spiced bread, typical of the Gemona del Friuli area, where it was traditionally prepared for the Christmas holidays. Each family had its own recipe, which was based on a mixture of Cinquantino corn flour (*sorc* in the Friulian language), rye, and wheat and enriched with dried fruit and flavorings. Baking always took place in the communal ovens of the villages or at the homes of wealthier families.

FRIULI-VENEZIA GIULIA

GUBANA

SWEET GUBANA EASTER BREAD

Makes 1 large round gubana, to be cut into 24 to 30 slices

INGREDIENTS

For the dough

20 g fresh brewer's yeast

200 g whole milk, warmed (about 100°F [38°C])

600 g pastry or cake flour, plus more for dusting

50 g sugar

3 eggs

5 g salt

100 g butter, at room temperature

1 egg white, beaten

For the filling

100 g walnuts, coarsely chopped

100 g pine nuts, coarsely chopped

70 g almonds, coarsely chopped

50 g sugar

50 g butter, at room temperature

100 g raisins

Grated zest of 1 orange

50 g amaretti cookies

50 g bread crumbs

60 g grappa, preferably, or apple brandy or pear brandy

Pinch of ground cinnamon

Pinch of ground nutmeg

RISE TIME

First rise: 2 hours

Proofing: 1 hour

BAKE TIME

40 to 50 minutes at 350°F (180°C)

1. Make the dough: In a small bowl, dissolve the brewer's yeast in the warm milk. In a large bowl, combine the flour with the milk mixture, sugar, eggs, salt, and butter.

2. Mix vigorously for about 10 minutes until you have a smooth, homogeneous mixture. Let rise in a bowl covered with a damp cloth, in a warm place, for about 2 hours or until doubled in volume.

3. Make the filling: In a large bowl, mix the coarsely chopped nuts, sugar, butter, raisins, grated orange zest, cookies, bread crumbs, grappa, cinnamon, and nutmeg. Mix the filling well until you have a smooth mixture, then set aside.

4. Roll out the dough on a floured surface, making a rectangle about 12 by 16 inches (30 by 41 cm). Spread the filling evenly on the dough, leaving a 1-inch (2.5 cm) border.

5. Roll the dough on itself from the longest side to make a log, seal the ends well, and form it into the shape of a snail.

6. Transfer the *gubana* to a baking sheet lined with parchment paper, cover with a dampened tea towel, and let rise again for about 1 hour or until doubled in volume.

7. Preheat the oven to 350°F (180°C). Brush the *gubana*, with the beaten egg white and bake for 40 to 50 minutes, until golden brown. Remove the oven and let cool completely on a wire rack before serving.

Did you know...

A dessert of Slovenian origin, *gubana* is typically associated with holy days and special occasions. In Gorizia and Trieste, the casing is made of short pastry, while in the Natisone valleys (Udine) it is made of yeast dough; the filling includes dried fruit, raisins, and other ingredients.

EMILIA-ROMAGNA

COPPIA FERRARESE

FERRARESE "COUPLE" SOURDOUGH BREAD

Makes 6 to 8 "couples"

INGREDIENTS

22 g salt
480 g water
1 kg pastry or cake flour, plus more for dusting
5 g diastatic malt powder
20 g fresh brewer's yeast
100 g lard

RISE TIME

Proofing: 2 hours at room temperature

BAKE TIME

20 minutes at 400°F (200°C)

1. In a large bowl, dissolve the salt in the water, add the flour, malt, and brewer's yeast, and start mixing, then add the lard and continue to work the dough vigorously—it will be very stiff, and it will take some effort to bring it together well—until the dough is as smooth as possible.

2. Turn the dough out onto a floured pastry board and roll it out with a rolling pin, then fold it in on itself and let it rest, wrapped in a sheet of plastic wrap, for about 10 minutes.

3. Divide the dough into balls weighing about 150 g. Flatten into long, narrow rectangles. Roll them on themselves from the narrow side, leaving a few inches (cm) at the end. Join them two by two, overlapping the remaining loose ends, then partially split them so that four small wedges are formed.

4. Lay the couplets on a floured baking dish and let them rise for about 2 hours at room temperature, covered with a tea towel.

5. Preheat the oven to 400°F (200°C) and bake for about 20 minutes, until golden brown.

Did you know...

Ciupèta is a hard bread of ancient tradition, particularly crispy and almost crumbless, characterized by the spiral shape of the long crescents that make it up, attached two by two. Its origins date back to the Carnival of 1536, on the occasion of a banquet organized for the Duke of Este. Since 2001, it boasts the Protected Geographical Indication label, and in 2004 a protection consortium was also established.

EMILIA-ROMAGNA

CHISOLA COI GRASEI

PORK CRACKLING BREAD

Makes 1 large sheet bread, about 13 by 18 inches (33 by 46 cm)

INGREDIENTS

For the poolish

300 g all-purpose flour

10 g fresh brewer's yeast

300 g warm water (about 110°F [43°C])

For the dough

700 g all-purpose flour

300 g water

22 g salt

30 g lard

20 g extra virgin olive oil

200 g pork cracklings

For finishing

Coarse salt

Chopped fresh rosemary (optional)

RISE TIME

First rise: 1 hour

Proofing: 2 hours

BAKE TIME

30 to 35 minutes at 400°F (200°C)

1. Make the poolish: Combine the flour, brewer's yeast, and warm water in a large bowl, then mix briefly until smooth. Cover the bowl with a damp tea towel and let rise in a warm place for 1 hour or until doubled in volume.

2. Make the dough: In a large bowl, mix the flour with the poolish. Add the water and salt and mix for about 10 more minutes. Add the lard and oil and knead until the dough is smooth. Add the pork cracklings (if you like a more intense flavor, you can also use seasoned ones) and gently mix until distributed evenly.

3. Cover the bowl with a dampened kitchen towel and let rise in a warm place for about 2 hours.

4. Lightly grease a baking sheet, lay the risen dough on it, and gently roll it out with your hands, to a thickness of less than 1 inch (2.5 cm).

5. Finish the dough: Poke holes all over the surface with your fingertips, then sprinkle with coarse salt and rosemary, if desired.

6. Preheat the oven to 400°F (200°C). Bake for 30 to 35 minutes or until golden brown.

Did you know...

Chisola coi grasei is a specialty of Val Tidone, in the province of Piacenza, where it was usually prepared for special occasions, such as festivals and celebrations. It is a soft and flavorful bread, enriched with crispy pork cracklings. It is delicious eaten hot or warm and goes best with a good glass of red wine or Malvasia dei Colli Piacentini.

RICCIOLA FERRARESE

FERRARESE BRIOCHE

Makes 20 to 24 brioche rings

INGREDIENTS

500 g butter
20 g sugar
26 g salt
500 g water
1 kg pastry or cake flour, sifted, plus more for dusting

RISE TIME

First rise: 2 hours
Second rise: 30 minutes
Third rise: 30 minutes
Fourth rise: 30 minutes
Fifth rise: Overnight (preferably)
Sixth rise: 30 minutes

BAKE TIME

30 minutes at 400°F (200°C)

1. Flatten the butter between two sheets of parchment paper.

2. Dissolve the sugar and salt in the water in a large bowl, then add the flour and mix until the dough is fairly smooth. Let it rest in the refrigerator for 2 hours.

3. Transfer the dough to a floured pastry board, roll it out well, and encase the butter in the center. Close by pinching the edges of the dough together, then roll it out with a rolling pin to a thickness of ⅓ inch (8 mm) and fold in four. Cover with plastic wrap and transfer to the refrigerator for 30 minutes.

4. Take the dough out of the refrigerator, roll it out to a thickness of ⅓ inch (8 mm), fold in four again, cover again with plastic wrap, and place in the refrigerator for another 30 minutes. Repeat this operation twice more: In total you will need to give the dough four folds of four. If possible, let it rest in the refrigerator overnight.

5. Roll out the dough to a thickness of ¼ inch (6 mm) and cut out strips 1 inch (2.5 cm) wide and 20 inches (51 cm) long. Twist and weave them together, forming ring-shaped loaves, then place them on a baking sheet lined with parchment paper and let rest in the refrigerator for 30 minutes.

6. Preheat the oven to 400°F (200°C) and bake for about 35 minutes, until golden brown.

Did you know...

Also called *ricciolina*, which means "curly," this bread is said to date back to the Renaissance: Its shape apparently recalls the hairstyle of women of the time. More likely, however, the *ricciola* made its appearance in city bakeries in more recent times, around the middle of the 20th century, as a way to reuse the day's leftover dough.

PANE SCIOCCO

TUSCAN UNSALTED BREAD

Makes 2 loaves

INGREDIENTS

1 kg all-purpose flour, plus more for dusting

550 g water

10 g fresh brewer's yeast

RISE TIME

First rise: 1 hour

Proofing: 2 hours

BAKE TIME

40 minutes at 425°F (220°C)

1. In a large bowl, mix the flour, water, and yeast until smooth. Transfer to a floured container, cover with a tea towel, and let rest for 1 hour at room temperature.

2. Turn the mixture out onto a pastry board, divide it into two loaves, and shape into elongated ovals. Place them on a floured tea towel and let them rise at room temperature for 2 hours.

3. Line a baking dish with parchment paper. Preheat the oven to 425°F (220°C). Lay the loaves in the baking dish or directly on a preheated refractory stone and bake until deep golden brown, about 40 minutes.

Did you know...

Produced in all Tuscan provinces, this bread is characterized by the absence of salt. This custom apparently dates back to the 12th century when, at the height of the rivalry between Pisa and Florence, the Pisans blocked the salt trade. When stale, the bread is a featured ingredient in numerous regional recipes such as *panzanella*, *acquacotta*, and *pappa al pomodoro*.

SCHIACCIATA
TUSCAN FOCACCIA

Makes 2 loaves

INGREDIENTS

800 g all-purpose flour, plus more for dusting
200 g white whole wheat flour
15 g fresh brewer's yeast
680 g water
50 g extra virgin olive oil, plus more for drizzling
20 g salt
Coarse salt, for sprinkling

RISE TIME

First rise: 2 hours
Second rise: 2 hours
Proofing: 30 minutes

BAKE TIME

20 minutes at 475°F (240°C)

1. In a large bowl, mix the all-purpose and whole wheat flours with the brewer's yeast and 600 g of the water. When the dough seems smooth, add the oil, salt, and remaining 80 g of water, and mix well to make a uniform dough. Transfer to a large bowl. Cover with a tea towel and let rest for 2 hours at room temperature.

2. Turn the dough out onto a lightly floured work surface and form two loaves. Arrange and spread each in a well-greased baking dish and let rise for 2 hours at room temperature. Press down the dough with your fingertips and let rise for another 30 minutes.

3. Preheat the oven to 475°F (240°C). Drizzle the surface with plenty of extra virgin oil, sprinkle with coarse salt, and bake for about 20 minutes, until golden brown.

Did you know...

Also commonly known as *Ciaccia* or focaccia, and usually square or rectangular, this bread is baked in the oven after being drizzled with a generous measure of Tuscan olive oil. Soft on the inside and with a nice crispy crust on the outside, it can be filled while still warm.

BUCCELLATO DI LUCCA

LUCCHESE SWEET ROLL

Makes 1 large circular loaf

INGREDIENTS

800 g pastry or cake flour
200 g all-purpose flour
600 g water
20 g fresh brewer's yeast
10 g salt
40 g extra virgin olive oil
150 g butter, at room temperature
10 g honey
50 g dried figs, chopped
50 g walnuts, chopped
100 g raisins, soaked in water until plump
50 g sugar, plus more for sprinkling
10 g anise seed
Grated zest of 1 lemon
1 egg, beaten

RISE TIME

First rise: 4 to 6 hours
Proofing: 1 hour

BAKE TIME

40 to 50 minutes at 350°F (180°C)

1. In a large bowl, add the flours, water, yeast, salt, and extra virgin olive oil and start working everything together. When the dough is firm (no longer sticky, but smooth and elastic), add the butter, honey, chopped figs, chopped walnuts, drained raisins, sugar, anise seeds, and grated lemon zest.

2. Mix vigorously for about 10 minutes to incorporate all the ingredients. If the dough seems too soft, add more flour, 1 tablespoon (7 g) at a time, until the desired consistency is reached.

3. Cover the bowl with a damp tea towel and let rise in a warm place for 4 to 6 hours, or until doubled in volume.

4. Form the dough into a ring-shaped loaf about 12 inches (30 cm) long. It should be 2 inches (5 cm) in diameter. Make a longitudinal incision across the entire surface of the bread, but do not go too deep.

5. Line a baking sheet with parchment paper. Place it on the prepared baking sheet and let it rise for 1 hour.

6. Preheat the oven to 350°F (180°C), brush the surface of the dough with beaten egg, sprinkle with sugar, and bake for 40 to 50 minutes. Take the *Buccellato* out of the oven once golden brown and let it cool completely on a wire rack before serving.

Did you know...

*Buccellato*is a sweet bread so deeply rooted in the region that a local saying goes like this: "He who comes to Lucca and doesn't eat *buccellato*is is as if he never came." Its origins date back to the Middle Ages, when it used to be prepared on the occasion of a child's confirmation, but today it can be bought year-round.

PAN NOCIATO
UMBRIAN WALNUT BREAD

Makes 2 loaves

INGREDIENTS

1 kg all-purpose flour, plus more for dusting

200 g solid sourdough starter (see page 76) (or 1¾ tablespoons [15 g] fresh brewer's yeast)

650 g water

10 g salt

3 g freshly ground pepper

20 g extra virgin olive oil

100 g grated pecorino-Romano cheese

200 g walnuts, chopped

RISE TIME

First rise: 1 hour

Proofing: Overnight in the refrigerator and 4 hours at room temperature

BAKE TIME

40 minutes at 400°F (200°C)

1. In a large bowl, mix the flour with the sourdough starter (or brewer's yeast) and 600 g of the water. When the mixture is sufficiently smooth, incorporate the salt, pepper, oil, remaining 50 g of water, and then the grated pecorino-Romano cheese and walnuts.

2. Let the mixture rise, covered with a tea towel, for 1 hour at room temperature.

3. Roll the dough out on a floured pastry board or clean surface, divide it into two loaves, and place them in a leavening basket or baking dish. Cover and refrigerate for 12 hours (overnight). Then, let the dough rise for 4 hours at room temperature.

4. Preheat the oven to 400°F (200°C) and bake for about 40 minutes, until golden brown.

Did you know...

Also known as *pan caciato* or *pane di San Martino*, *pan nociato* falls into the large category of traditional Italian non-sweet desserts and is widespread throughout the region, especially in the province of Perugia. Of ancient origins (in the 16th century a treatise codified its production standards), it is prepared mainly in the fall and for winter holidays. The traditional recipe calls for walnuts, grated pecorino-Romano cheese from Norcia, extra virgin olive oil, salt, and pepper to be added to the bread dough. From village to village, you'll find small variations like the addition of raisins or red wine.

TORTA AL TESTO
UMBRIAN FLATBREAD

Makes 2 large flatbread rounds

INGREDIENTS

1 kg all-purpose flour or white spelt flour

5 g baking soda

20 g salt

40 g extra virgin olive oil

500 g warm water (about 100°F [38°C])

RISE TIME

First rise: 30 minutes

BAKE TIME

2 to 3 minutes each side

1. Combine the flour and baking soda in a large bowl, then add the salt, extra virgin olive oil, and warm water. Mix vigorously for about 10 minutes, until a smooth dough forms.

2. Cover the bowl with a dampened tea towel and let it rest at room temperature for about 30 minutes.

3. Heat a *testo* pan over medium-high heat; if you do not have one, you can use a nonstick cast-iron skillet or griddle.

4. Divide the dough into two equal parts and roll each one out on a floured work surface, forming two disks about 10 inches (26 cm) in diameter and ⅓ inch (8 mm) thick.

5. Cook each disk on the hot *testo* for 2 to 3 minutes per side, until golden brown, and allow to cool slightly before serving.

Did you know...

Umbrians also call this bread *crescia* or *focaccia schiacciata* and it is still one of the symbols of the regional culinary tradition. It is a kind of focaccia or flatbread baked on the *testo*, a round, cast-iron plate. Prepared with a few simple ingredients, it is very versatile: It can be enjoyed alone as bread or stuffed with salumi, cheeses, vegetables, or anything else that you like. You can also flavor the dough with herbs like rosemary and sage and, for a crisper texture, extend the cooking time by 1 minute per side.

ROCCIATA
UMBRIAN FRUIT BREAD

Makes 1 large round bread, to be cut into 24 to 30 slices

INGREDIENTS

For the dough

- 1 kg pastry or cake flour, plus more for dusting
- 500 g water
- 10 g fresh brewer's yeast, crumbled
- 20 g salt
- 40 g extra virgin olive oil

For the filling

- 50 g raisins
- 20 g rum
- 50 g dried figs, chopped
- 100 g walnuts, chopped
- 20 g pine nuts
- 50 g candied fruit
- Grated zest of 1 lemon
- 5 g unsweetened cocoa powder
- 5 g ground cinnamon
- 10 g anise seeds, soaked in water for 10 minutes

For the finishing

- Alchermes or amaretto liqueur
- Confectioners' sugar

RISE TIME

First rise: 4 to 6 hours

Proofing: 2 hours

BAKE TIME

50 minutes at 350°F (180°C)

1. Make the dough: In a large bowl, mix the flour with the water, crumbled brewer's yeast, salt, and extra virgin olive oil. Work everything vigorously for about 10 minutes until the dough is smooth and well mixed.
2. Cover the bowl with a damp tea towel and let rise in a warm place for 4 to 6 hours, or until doubled in volume.
3. Make the filling: Soak the raisins in the rum for 5 minutes, then drain and add the chopped figs and nuts, candied fruit, grated lemon zest, cocoa, cinnamon, and presoaked anise seeds.
4. When the dough has risen, turn it out onto a floured work surface and roll it out with a rolling pin, making a rectangle about 2 inches (5 cm) thick. Arrange the filling evenly on top, leaving 2 inches (5 cm) from the edge, then roll the dough and form a spiral.
5. Transfer to a baking sheet lined with parchment paper and let rise for 2 hours at room temperature.
6. Preheat the oven to 350°F (180°C) and bake for about 50 minutes.
7. Finish the bread: In a small bowl, combine the Alchermes and confectioners' sugar into a thick, creamy icing.
8. Take the *rocciata* out of the oven, drizzle it with the prepared icing, and let it cool on a wire rack.

Did you know...

Typical of the Christmas and All Saints' Day festivities (but today it can be found commercially at any time of year), *rocciata* is a sweet bread found mainly in the area from Assisi to Foligno, in the province of Perugia. Its crumbly crust makes it irresistible, while the generous filling of walnuts, raisins, candied fruit, and spices consecrates it as a true jewel of Umbrian pastry.

MARCHE

PANE DI FARRO

FARRO BREAD

Makes 2 medium-large loaves

INGREDIENTS

500 g white farro (or spelt) flour
500 g whole grain spelt flour
150 g solid sourdough starter (see page 76) (or 1 tablespoon [8 g] fresh brewer's yeast)
680 g water
20 g salt

RISE TIME

First rise: Overnight in the refrigerator
Proofing: 4 hours

BAKE TIME

40 minutes at 425°F (220°C)

1. In a large bowl, mix the two flours together. Slowly add the sourdough starter and 600 g of the water and knead. Once combined, incorporate the salt and the remaining 80 g of water and continue to knead vigorously until it is smooth and homogeneous.

2. Transfer the dough to a clean bowl, cover with plastic wrap, and let rise in the refrigerator overnight.

3. Divide the dough into two parts and shape each into an elongated loaf, as you see in the photo. Place the loaves in a leavening basket or baking dish, score along the top, and let rise for 4 hours at room temperature.

4. Preheat the oven to 425°F (220°C). Bake the loaves directly on a hot stone or on a baking sheet lined with parchment paper for about 40 minutes, or until golden brown.

Did you know...

Farro, an ancient grain family including spelt, is a cereal that has been rooted in the Marche region since ancient times. In fact, it was one of the symbols of the early Picenian civilization, and the ritual of *confarreation* that was practiced there—the exchange of a tribute between the families of betrothed couples—was named after this food. The bread made from it has a fairly dark color and is characterized by its aroma and rustic flavor.

PIZZA ROSSINI

ROSSINI PIZZA

Makes 6 pizzas

INGREDIENTS

For the dough

1 kg all-purpose flour, plus more for dusting

5 g fresh brewer's yeast

600 g water

25 g salt

50 g extra virgin olive oil

For the topping

Extra virgin olive oil

Tomato puree

Shredded mozzarella

Sliced hard-boiled eggs

Mayonnaise

RISE TIME

First rise: 1 hour

Second rise: Overnight in the refrigerator

Proofing: 3 hours

BAKE TIME

8 to 10 minutes at 475°F (240°C)

1. Make the dough: In a large bowl, mix the flour with the yeast, then add the water and knead. When you get a fairly smooth consistency, add the salt and oil and continue to work everything together well. Cover with a damp tea towel and let rise at room temperature for 1 hour.

2. Divide the dough into six balls. Place in an airtight container and let rest in the refrigerator overnight.

3. Let the dough balls rise for 3 hours at room temperature.

4. Top the pizzas: Roll each ball out on a floured surface into a round disk, drizzle some olive oil over the surface, and top with the tomato puree and shredded mozzarella.

5. Preheat the oven to 475°F (240°C). Bake the pizzas one at a time on a refractory stone, pizza stone, or baking sheet for 8 to 10 minutes, until the cheese is melted and bubbly. Remove from the oven, top with the sliced hard-boiled eggs, and drizzle with mayonnaise. Serve immediately.

Did you know...

This dish is nothing more than a simple margherita pizza topped with slices of hard-boiled eggs and mayonnaise—this is how the people of Pesaro like to eat pizza. The combination was apparently invented by a now-closed bakery in the Marche town in the 1960s. The pizza's name is a tribute to the well-known composer and fellow citizen, Gioacchino Rossini.

CIAMBELLE STROZZOSE

EASTER ANISE BREAD

Makes 12 *ciambelle strozzose*

INGREDIENTS

5 large eggs
100 g sugar
25 g extra virgin olive oil
Grated zest of 1 lemon
500 g all-purpose flour, plus more for mixing
90 g Mistrà (or any other anise liqueur)
20 g baking soda
2.5 g salt

RISE TIME

First rise: At least 4 hours (ideally overnight)

COOK TIME

First phase: 10 minutes in boiling water

Second phase: 15 minutes at 400°F (200°C) and then 30 to 35 minutes at 350°F (180°C)

1. Using a stand mixer or hand mixer, beat the eggs and sugar on medium speed until combined. With the mixer on, add the oil and grated lemon zest. Reduce the mixer speed to low and gradually add the flour.

2. Mix the liqueur with a little bit of flour in a glass before incorporating it into the dough—this way you will not run the risk of blocking the rising. Mix everything together and then dust the mixture with the baking soda and salt.

3. Mix once more until the mixture is smooth and easy to work with your hands, then divide it into a dozen portions and make ring-shaped rounds with a hole in the middle.

4. Fill a large pot with water, bring it to a boil over high heat, and boil the *ciambelle*, one at a time, for about 10 minutes, turning them occasionally. Once golden, use a skimmer to transfer them to a wire rack. Allow them to cool slightly, then slit them down middle lengthwise and let them rest for at least 4 hours (although ideally, they should rest overnight, as per tradition).

5. Preheat the oven to 400°F (200°C). Place the rings on a baking sheet lined with parchment paper and bake for 15 minutes, then lower the temperature to 350°F (180°C) and leave them in the oven for another 30 to 35 minutes. They are ready when they are nice and golden on the surface. You can eat them as they are, freshly made, or frost them with melted chocolate or icing and top them with colored sprinkles.

Did you know...

Popular throughout the Marche region, with some small local variations, these *ciambelle* are a typical regional Easter dessert. They are characterized by their anise aroma, imparted by the Mistrà liqueur. In many villages they represent the classic Easter outing treat; however, Holy Thursday is the day when they are still baked the most in homes and artisan bakeries. The curious name (*strozzose* can be roughly translated as "stranglers") apparently refers to their consistency, which is rather dry, such that they are best enjoyed with a glass of wine.

CIRIOLA
CLASSIC LAZIO ROLL

Makes 10 to 12 rolls

INGREDIENTS

For the *biga* (starter)
500 g all-purpose flour, plus more for dusting
5 g fresh brewer's yeast
250 g water

For the dough
330 g water
5 g fresh brewer's yeast
5 g diastatic malt powder
500 g white whole wheat flour
22 g salt

RISE TIME

First rise: 18 hours at 64°F (18°C)
Second rise: 1 hour at room temperature
Proofing: 1 hour

BAKE TIME

12 minutes at 475°F (240°C)

1. Make the *biga*: In a large bowl, mix the flour with the brewer's yeast and water. Once a shaggy dough forms, cover with plastic wrap and let rise for 18 hours in a cool part of the house (the ideal temperature is 64°F [18°C]).

2. Make the dough: Place the risen *biga* and some of the water in the bowl of a stand mixer or a large bowl. Mix, then add the brewer's yeast, malt, a little more water, and flour. Mix until smooth and homogeneous, then incorporate the salt and remaining water and mix for a few more minutes. Cover with plastic wrap and let rise for 1 hour at room temperature.

3. Divide the dough into 10 to 12 small loaves. Now take the dough and fold it over on itself, forming a kind of rhombus (i.e., a small loaf elongated at the ends like a croissant). Press on the ends and flatten it like a tongue. Using the long edge, roll the dough into a log. Flatten it again and fold it back on itself, rolling the long edge to create a log. Pinch the ends to create tips.

4. Place the *ciriolas* on a baking sheet lined with parchment paper, then cover with a tea towel and let rise at room temperature until doubled (this will take 1 hour or so).

5. Dust the surface of the *ciriolas* with a little flour and make a cut on each one lengthwise. Preheat the oven to 475°F (240°C) and bake for 12 minutes, or until golden brown.

Did you know...

The *ciriola* is the most classic of Lazio breads, included in the list of certified traditional regional food products. It has an elongated shape and a bulge in the central part, a soft crumb, and a crispy, golden crust with a characteristic split. As for the etymology of the name, there are several theses, but the most widely accepted one claims it derives from the vague resemblance to a small eel (also called a *ciriola* in Italian) that was once commonly found in the waters of the Tiber.

TEGLIA ALLA ROMANA

ROMAN PAN PIZZA

Makes 2 pizzas

INGREDIENTS

1 kg white whole wheat flour, plus more for dusting
7 g fresh brewer's yeast
780 g water
22 g salt
40 g extra virgin olive oil

RISE TIME

First rise: 12 hours in the refrigerator
Proofing: 3 hours

BAKE TIME

15 minutes at 475°F (240°C)

1. In a large bowl, mix the flour, yeast, and 750 g of the water. Mix until a smooth dough forms, about 10 minutes. Add the salt, oil, and remaining 30 g of water, and continue mixing until it is completely absorbed by the mass. Let it rise in the refrigerator for about 12 hours.

2. Divide into two balls and let them rise for 3 more hours at room temperature.

3. Roll the balls out on a floured surface, forming them into rectangular shapes, then place them in baking pans (12 by 16 inches [30 by 41 cm]).

4. Preheat the oven to 475°F (240°C) with a rack in the middle position and a rack near the top. Bake for 8 minutes on the middle rack and 7 minutes on the rack near the top. If you have a pizza oven or wood-fired oven, the ideal baking is at 550°F (288°C) for 8 minutes.

5. Take the pizzas out of the oven, let them cool just slightly, then cut them in half lengthwise and top them with the ingredients of your choice.

Did you know...

A timeless Roman street food, pan pizza is characterized by a low, crunchy, high-hydration dough.

CROSTATA DI VISCIOLE E RICOTTA

SOUR CHERRY AND RICOTTA CHEESECAKE

Makes one 9-inch (23 cm) cheesecake

INGREDIENTS

For the pastry

500 g butter, softened
500 g sugar
Grated zest of 1 lemon
5 g salt
4 large eggs
1 kg all-purpose flour
15 g baking powder

For the filling

500 g sheep's milk ricotta cheese
100 g sugar
400 g sour cherries

RISE TIME

First rise: Overnight in the refrigerator

BAKE TIME

50 minutes at 325°F (160°C)

1. Make the pastry one day in advance: In a stand mixer fitted with a paddle attachment, mix the butter, sugar, lemon zest, and salt, then slowly add the eggs and continue working the mixture until it is firm. Finally, in a large bowl, sift together the flour and baking powder. Slowly incorporate the dry ingredients into the wet ingredients.

2. When you have a smooth and homogeneous dough, form it into a ball and wrap it with plastic wrap, then let it rise overnight in the refrigerator.

3. Make the filling: The next day, strain the ricotta in a colander, place it in a bowl, and mix it with the sugar until creamy. Take the dough again, divide it into two parts—one larger than the other—and roll each one out with a rolling pin until it is about ⅛ to ¼ inch (3 to 6 mm) thick.

4. Grease a 9-inch (23 cm) round baking pan with butter or line it with parchment paper. Add the larger disk and spread the sour cherries on top. Next, spread the ricotta cream, level the surface, and cover with the other disk of short crust pastry, sealing the edges well. Score the top pastry with an elongated diamond pattern.

5. Preheat the oven to 325°F (160°C) and bake for about 50 minutes, until golden brown.

Did you know...

This irresistible dessert is part of the Roman Jewish culinary tradition and is composed of a short crust pastry shell topped with a soft filling made of ricotta cheese, sugar and preserves of *visciole* which are wild, sour cherries, dark in color and with a pleasantly sour flavor and are very common in the Lazio region.

PANE ALLE PATATE
POTATO BREAD

Makes 2 loaves

INGREDIENTS

1 kg white whole wheat flour, plus more for dusting

300 g solid sourdough starter (see page 76) (or 8 g fresh brewer's yeast)

640 g water

10 g salt

30 g extra virgin olive oil

200 g potatoes, peeled, diced, and blanched in boiling water for 4 minutes

RISE TIME

First rise: 2 hours at room temperature

Proofing: 4 hours

BAKE TIME

40 minutes at 425°F (220°C)

1. In a large bowl, mix the flour with the sourdough starter and 600 g of the water until you have a fairly smooth dough, then add the remaining 40 g of water, salt, and oil, continue mixing, and then incorporate the diced potatoes.

2. Transfer the dough to a clean bowl, cover with a tea towel, and let it rise for 2 hours at room temperature.

3. Turn the dough out onto a floured pastry board and divide it into two round-shaped loaves. Place them in a proofing basket and let rise for 4 hours.

4. Preheat the oven to 425°F (220°C). Arrange the loaves on a baking sheet lined with parchment paper and bake, with plenty of steam (see Note), for about 40 minutes, until the surface is golden and crispy.

Note: To make steam in your oven, bring a medium, ovenproof pot of water to a boil over medium-high heat. Meanwhile, preheat the oven with one rack in the lowest position and one in the middle. Add the pot to the lowest rack of the oven and your bread to the middle rack.

Did you know...

This bread, characteristic of the inland and mountainous areas of Abruzzo, was born out of the need to save flour, partly replacing it with the more economical potatoes. Distinguished by its crisp crust and soft, moist interior, it keeps well for up to a week.

ABRUZZO

PIZZA SCIMA
UNLEAVENED PIZZA

Makes 1 large pizza

INGREDIENTS

1 kg pastry or cake flour
5 g baking soda
20 g salt
500 g dry white wine
100 g extra virgin olive oil, plus more for brushing

RISE TIME

First rise: 30 minutes

BAKE TIME

30 to 40 minutes at 350°F (180°C)

1. Place the flour, baking soda, and salt in a large bowl, then gradually add the white wine and extra virgin olive oil, stirring with a fork so that you have a sandy mixture. Work the mixture vigorously with your hands for 10 to 15 minutes. Once a smooth and homogeneous dough ball has formed, cover it with a damp cloth and let it rise at room temperature for 30 minutes.

2. Preheat the oven to 350°F (180°C) and line a baking sheet with baking paper.

3. Roll out the dough in a baking sheet with a rolling pin, making a disk about ¼ to ¾ inch (6 mm to 2 cm) thick.

4. Using a knife, make diamond-shaped incisions in the surface of the pizza and brush it with extra virgin olive oil. Bake for 30 to 40 minutes, or until golden brown, then remove it from the oven and let it cool before serving.

Did you know...

Also known as unleavened pizza because of the absence of yeast in the dough, this is a focaccia typical of the Abruzzo peasant tradition. Its origins date back to the late Middle Ages, when several Israelite communities settled in the region. Thin and crunchy, it can be eaten, as an alternative to bread, alone or accompanied with salumi, cheeses, grilled vegetables, and other regional specialties.

PARROZZO

Makes 1 medium-large cake

INGREDIENTS

For the dough

- 100 g peeled almonds
- 5 eggs
- 130 g sugar
- 100 g durum wheat semolina
- 60 g butter, melted
- 40 g Amaretto (or other flavored liqueur)
- Grated zest of 1 lemon

For the topping

- 200 g dark chocolate
- 20 g butter

BAKE TIME

40 to 50 minutes at 350°F (180°C)

1. Make the dough: Finely chop the almonds; break the eggs and separate the yolks from the egg whites. In a large bowl, beat the yolks with the sugar to a light and frothy mixture, then add the semolina, chopped almonds, melted butter, liqueur, and grated lemon zest, mixing well to combine all the ingredients.

2. In a separate bowl, beat the egg whites until stiff and gently incorporate them into the yolk mixture, in a bottom-up motion so as not to deflate the egg whites.

3. Preheat the oven to 350°F (180°C). Grease and flour a cone-shaped Bundt pan mold, pour in the mixture, and level it well. Bake for 40 to 50 minutes, or until golden brown.

4. Meanwhile, prepare the topping: Finely chop the dark chocolate and melt it in a small saucepan in a double boiler together with the butter, stirring continuously until you have a smooth, homogeneous ganache.

5. Remove the *parrozzo* from the oven and let it cool completely. Spread the ganache over the cake, coating it completely, and put it in the refrigerator for 1 hour or so for the chocolate to set.

Did you know...

This almond-based *zuccotto*, with a mouthwatering dark chocolate coating, is the typical Abruzzo Christmas dessert, especially in the Pescarese area. Its origins hark back to coarse bread, made with cornmeal, so called to contrast it with white flour bread, reserved for the wealthier classes. The recipe we know today—which takes the shape of that bread—is a relatively recent creation. It was in fact the Pescara baker Luigi D'Amico who invented it and registered the trademark in 1926; he himself sent a specimen of the product to the Vittoriale, asking Gabriele D'Annunzio to give it his blessing. The poet, enraptured, sang its praises in his famous verses.

TARALLI DI VENAFRO

VENAFRO TARALLI

Makes 8 medium bread rings

INGREDIENTS

1 kg durum wheat semolina
10 g fresh brewer's yeast
20 g salt
400 g water, plus more for brushing
200 g extra virgin olive oil
Fennel seeds (optional)

RISE TIME

First rise: 2 hours
Proofing: 45 minutes

BAKE TIME

20 minutes at 350°F (180°C)

1. Combine the flour and brewer's yeast in a large bowl, then add the salt, water, and oil. Mix vigorously for about 10 minutes until you have a smooth, homogeneous dough. Cover it with a damp tea towel and let it rise at room temperature for about 2 hours, or until doubled in volume.

2. Divide the dough into 8 portions and roll each into a log about 8 inches (20 cm) long. Twist each log and join the ends together to form irregular ring-shaped loaves.

3. Arrange the *taralli* on a baking sheet lined with parchment paper, brush the surface with water, and, if you like, sprinkle with fennel seeds. Let rise for another 45 minutes at room temperature.

4. Preheat the oven to 350°F (180°C). Bake the *taralli* for about 20 minutes, or until golden brown, then take them out of the oven and let them cool.

Did you know...

Also known as biscotti or *v'scuott*, these are rustic, crumbly *taralli* originating in Venafro. Apparently, the peculiar shape originated in the 18th century when bakers began to salvage the remains of bread dough by making twisted rings. Their goodness is due to the use of simple and natural ingredients, among which extra virgin olive oil stands out (if you like, you can also use one with a strong flavor). Stored in an airtight container, *taralli* keep well for several days.

PIZZA MOLISANA DI SAN MARTINO

SAINT MARTIN'S FOCACCIA

Makes 2 loaves

INGREDIENTS

1 kg pastry or cake flour
25 g fresh brewer's yeast
500 g whole milk
200 g grated pecorino-Romano or Parmigiano Reggiano cheese
10 g salt
5 g freshly ground pepper
100 g extra virgin olive oil, plus more for brushing

RISE TIME

First rise: 30 minutes at room temperature
Proofing: 2 hours at room temperature

BAKE TIME

30 to 40 minutes at 350°F (180°C)

1. In a large bowl, mix the flour with the yeast, milk, and grated cheese for about 10 minutes. Then add the salt, pepper, and oil and continue to work everything together so that you have a smooth, homogeneous dough. Cover the bowl with a damp tea towel and let rise at room temperature for about 30 minutes.

2. Line a baking sheet with parchment paper. Divide the dough in half and shape into two round loaves on the prepared baking sheet. Let rise at room temperature for 2 hours.

3. Preheat the oven to 350°F (180°C). Use a knife to make a star-shaped incision in the surface of the dough and brush with oil.

4. Bake for 30 to 40 minutes, or until the loaves are golden brown.

Did you know...

This focaccia from the Molise culinary tradition, particularly from the Campobasso area, is prepared on November 11, the feast of St. Martin, and is a symbol of abundance and prosperity.

CEPPELLIATE

BLACK CHERRY CRESCENT COOKIES

Makes 20 to 24 crescent cookies

INGREDIENTS

1 kg all-purpose flour
16 g baking powder
400 g sugar
3 g salt
Grated zest of 1 lemon
200 g almonds, chopped
500 g cold lard or butter
5 eggs
100 g white wine
Black cherry jam
Ground cinnamon

RISE TIME

First rise: 30 minutes in the refrigerator

BAKE TIME

15 to 20 minutes at 350°F (180°C)

1. In a large bowl, combine the flour with the baking powder, then add the sugar, salt, grated lemon zest, and chopped almonds (for a stronger flavor, you can also toast them beforehand) and mix well.

2. Incorporate the cold lard in batches, working the mixture with your fingers until you get a sandy dough.

3. Add the eggs and wine, mixing vigorously. Once a smooth, homogeneous dough has formed, cover with a damp cloth and let rise in the refrigerator for at least 30 minutes.

4. Preheat the oven to 350°F (180°C).

5. Roll the dough out with a rolling pin. Using a pastry cutter, cut out circles, place a little jam in the center of each, and close to form a crescent, sealing the edges well.

6. Lay the cookies on a baking sheet lined with parchment paper and bake for 15 to 20 minutes. Sprinkle them with cinnamon while they are still warm, then let cool.

Did you know...

Crumbly, with an intense flavor of almonds and cinnamon, *"c'pp'liat"* are never missing from the tables set by families in the village of Trivento, in the province of Campobasso, during the Christmas season. The traditional recipe calls for the use of a special iron mold that gives the cookies their typical shape. They keep well for up to 4 days if stored in an airtight container.

PANE PUGLIESE
PUGLIESE SOURDOUGH BREAD

Makes 2 loaves

INGREDIENTS

1 kg twice-milled durum wheat semolina

660 g water

200 g refreshed solid sourdough starter (see page 76) (or 2½ teaspoons [7 g] fresh brewer's yeast)

24 g salt

RISE TIME

First rise: Overnight in the refrigerator

Proofing: 2 hours

BAKE TIME

40 minutes at 425°F (220°C)

1. In a large bowl, mix the semolina with 600 g of the water and the sourdough starter until smooth, then add the remaining 60 g of water and salt and work again until you have a uniform loaf.

2. Put it in a large bowl, cover with plastic wrap, place it in the refrigerator, and let it rise overnight.

3. The next day, divide the dough into two parts and form two round loaves. Place them on a baking sheet covered with parchment paper and let them rise for 2 hours.

4. Preheat the oven to 425°F (220°C).

5. Just before you are ready to bake, score the loaves crosswise, making two crosscuts. Bake with plenty of steam (see Note) for about 40 minutes.

Note: To make steam in your oven, bring a medium, ovenproof pot of water to a boil over medium-high heat. Meanwhile, preheat the oven with one rack in the lowest position and one in the middle. Add the pot to the lowest rack of the oven and your bread to the middle rack.

Did you know...

Typically large, made with twice-milled durum wheat semolina and sourdough, this bread from Puglia was the first to cross regional borders, becoming highly valued and sought after throughout Italy.

FOCACCIA PUGLIESE

PUGLIESE FOCACCIA

Makes 3 focaccia

INGREDIENTS

For the dough

600 g all-purpose flour
400 g durum wheat semolina
10 g fresh brewer's yeast
5 g diastatic malt powder
700 g water
25 g salt
100 g extra virgin olive oil

For the garnish

Cherry tomatoes, cut in half
Baresana olives or Castelvetrano olives
Extra virgin olive oil
Salt
Oregano

RISE TIME

First rise: 2 hours
Second rise: 30 minutes
Proofing: 1 hour

BAKE TIME

18 to 20 minutes at 475°F (240°C)

1. Make the dough: Mix the flour and semolina with the yeast, malt powder, and 600 g of the water in a large bowl. When the dough is smooth enough, add the remaining 100 g of water, then add the salt and finally the oil. Transfer to a pastry board and knead until you get a soft, silky mass. Let rise for 2 hours at room temperature.

2. Divide the dough into three balls. Spread each focaccia in a well-greased 8-inch (20 cm) baking pan and let rise for 30 minutes at room temperature.

3. Garnish the dough: Spread the dough slightly with your fingers and top with the cherry tomatoes (the skin should be facing up and the flesh down), the olives, and generous amount of extra virgin olive oil. Let rise one last time for 1 hour at room temperature.

4. Preheat the oven to 475°F (240°C). Just before you are ready to bake, sprinkle the focaccia with salt and bake for 18 to 20 minutes, until the surface is nicely browned.

5. Sprinkle the focaccia with plenty of oregano after you've taken it out of the oven. Serve immediately.

Did you know...

Focaccia is one of the gastronomic icons of Puglia, so much so that as you travel around the region, you may come across many different ways of preparing it. Often boiled potatoes are also included in the dough, giving it particular softness. Perfect in its simplicity, it can be enjoyed at any time of the day.

OCCHI DI SANTA LUCIA

SAINT LUCY'S EYES / SWEET TARALLI

Makes 48 to 60 cookies

INGREDIENTS

For the dough

1 kg pastry or cake flour, plus more for dusting

5 g salt

300 g extra virgin olive oil

300 g dry white wine

3 large eggs

Grated zest of 1 lemon

1 teaspoon ground cinnamon

½ teaspoon anise seed

For the glaze

100 g confectioners' sugar

1 egg white

RISE TIME

First rise: 30 minutes in the refrigerator

BAKE TIME

15 to 20 minutes at 350°F (180°C)

1. Make the dough: Put the flour in a large bowl together with the salt. Add the extra virgin oil, wine, eggs, grated lemon zest, cinnamon, and anise seeds (for a stronger flavor, you can lightly toast them before adding them). Mix vigorously until smooth and homogeneous; if it is too soft, add more flour, 1 tablespoon (7 g) at a time.

2. Cover the dough ball with a damp tea towel and let rise in the refrigerator for at least 30 minutes.

3. Preheat the oven to 350°F (180°C) and line a baking sheet with parchment paper.

4. Roll out the dough on a floured work surface until it is about ⅓ inch (8 mm) thick. Cut strips from the dough and overlap the two ends so that they form small *tarallini,* as shown in the photo.

5. Arrange them on the prepared baking sheet and bake for 15 to 20 minutes, or until golden brown. Remove from the oven and transfer to a wire rack to cool completely.

6. In the meantime, prepare the icing: In a small bowl, mix the confectioners' sugar with the egg white until smooth and thick.

7. Decorate the cooled cookies with the icing using a teaspoon. Let dry before serving.

Did you know...

These traditional sweet *tarallini* from Puglia are prepared on December 13, the feast day of St. Lucy, patron saint of eyesight, and, more generally, throughout the Christmas season. The flavor is delicate, characterized by a pleasant anise aroma and a crumbly texture. The round shape, with a hole in the center, is reminiscent of an eye, hence the name *occhi di Santa Lucia, or* St. Lucy's eyes. After baking, the cookies are covered with a white icing made of egg white and confectioners' sugar.

PANE CAFONE
NEAPOLITAN PEASANT BREAD

Makes 2 loaves

INGREDIENTS

800 g all-purpose flour, plus more for dusting

200 g natural stone-ground whole wheat flour

300 g solid sourdough starter (see page 76) (or 3½ teaspoons [10 g] fresh brewer's yeast)

700 g water

25 g salt

RISE TIME

First rise: 1 hour

Proofing: Overnight in the refrigerator

BAKE TIME

40 minutes at 425°F (220°C)

1. In a bowl, mix the two flours with the sourdough starter and 600 g of the water until you have a fairly smooth consistency. Add the salt—if you are using brewer's yeast, add another 5 g—and the remaining 100 g of water and mix vigorously until you obtain a soft, homogeneous dough. Cover the bowl with plastic wrap. Allow the dough to rise at room temperature for about 1 hour.

2. Turn the dough out onto a floured pastry board and shape into two loaves. Place them on a well-floured tea towel and transfer them to the refrigerator overnight.

3. The following day, preheat the oven to 425°F (220°C). Take the loaves out of the refrigerator and bake them directly on a hot oven stone (or on a baking sheet) for about 40 minutes, until dark golden brown.

Did you know...

Among the symbols of Campania's famous breads, this one with its dark, crispy crust and high, beautifully honeycombed crumb has peasant origins. The name apparently comes from *ca' fune*, because the men charged with bringing it to Naples came down from the slopes of Vesuvius tied with ropes (*funi*), which were also used to keep them from getting lost in the city. Cafone can be prepared in various shapes: the *cocchia* (long and flattened), the *pagnotta* (round and flattened), of the *palatone* (a rather high parallelepiped with rounded ends).

PANUOZZO DI GRAGNANO
CAMPANIAN SANDWICH ROLL

Makes 2 sandwiches

INGREDIENTS

For the dough

1 kg pastry or cake flour
7 g fresh brewer's yeast
700 g water
22 g salt
20 g extra virgin olive oil

For the filling

Extra virgin olive oil
Freshly ground pepper
Smoked pancetta or bacon
Buffalo mozzarella
Grilled eggplant

RISE TIME

First rise: 2 hours
Second rise: 3 hours

BAKE TIME

10 to 12 minutes at 475°F (240°C)

1. Make the dough: Place the flour in a large bowl. Dissolve the yeast in the water. Add the yeast, water, salt, and oil, then mix vigorously for about 10 minutes until a smooth, homogeneous dough ball forms. If the dough is too soft, gradually incorporate more flour.

2. Cover the dough with a damp cloth and let it rise in a warm place for about 2 hours, or until doubled in volume.

3. Divide the dough into two equal parts and let them rise for 3 hours at room temperature. After this time, spread them with your hands, forming two oval disks about 12 inches (30 cm) long and 8 inches (20 cm) wide.

4. Preheat the oven to 475°F (240°C). Bake the *panuozzi* on a hot stone, if possible, for 10 to 12 minutes, then remove them from the oven and let cool.

5. Fill the rolls: Cut them in half lengthwise with a serrated knife and spread the fillings evenly.

6. In addition to the suggested fillings, I recommend you try the *panuozzo* with roasted pork, fresh *fior di latte* mozzarella cheese, and sweet *cruschi* peppers in oil.

Did you know...

Panuozzo is a fairly recent invention. In fact, this Campanian street food originated in the 1980s in Gragnano, the city of pasta, as an alternative to pizza. It is distinguished by its irregular oval shape and crispy crust and can be filled with a wide variety of ingredients.

CAMPANIA

RUM BABÀ

Makes 18 to 20 babà

INGREDIENTS

For the dough

1 kg pastry or cake flour
15 g brewer's yeast
75 g sugar
15 eggs
18 g salt
200 g butter, softened

For the syrup

100 g water
150 g sugar
80 g rum

RISE TIME

First rise: 4 hours at room temperature

BAKE TIME

20 to 25 minutes at 350°F (180°C)

1. Make the dough: In the bowl of the stand mixer fitted with the paddle attachment, combine the flour, brewer's yeast, sugar, and 10 of the eggs. Mix on medium speed until a shaggy dough forms. With the mixer still on, slowly incorporate the salt, the remaining 5 eggs, and then the butter.

2. Transfer the dough to the work surface and form balls, then place in the special 3.1-ounce buttered babà molds. Let rise for 4 hours at room temperature, away from drafts.

3. Preheat the oven to 350°F (180°C). Bake for 20 to 25 minutes, or until golden brown.

4. Make the syrup: Heat the water and sugar in a medium saucepan, constantly whisking until dissolved, about 5 minutes. Add the rum and remove from the heat.

5. Take the babas out of the oven and let them cool. Remove them from the molds and dip them completely into the still-warm syrup until they are well soaked. Take them out, squeeze them lightly, and set them to drain on a wire rack.

6. If you like, you can split them in half and fill with cream or custard.

Did you know...

Perhaps not everyone knows that the symbol of Neapolitan confectionery art actually originated in Poland. In fact, it arrived in the Kingdom of Naples only in the 19th century, through French court cooks who had adopted it, in turn, from the favorite recipes of Polish king Stanislaus I.

STRAZZATA DI AVIGLIANO
AVIGLIANO SOURDOUGH BREAD

Makes 2 loaves

INGREDIENTS

600 g twice-milled durum wheat semolina (Senatore Cappelli variety, if possible), plus more for dusting
400 g bread flour
100 g solid sourdough starter (see page 76) (or ¾ teaspoon [2 g] fresh brewer's yeast)
20 g salt
5 g freshly ground pepper
700 g warm water (about 100°F [38°C])
Extra virgin olive oil (optional)

RISE TIME

First rise: 2 hours
Proofing: 8 to 10 hours

BAKE TIME

25 to 30 minutes at 400°F (200°C)

1. Combine the semolina and bread flour in a large bowl. Add the sourdough starter, salt, and pepper. Gradually add the warm water, stirring with a spoon until you have a fairly smooth dough.

2. Transfer the mixture to a floured work surface and continue kneading for about 10 minutes, until you have a smooth dough. If it is too soft, incorporate some more flour, 1 tablespoon (8 g) at a time.

3. Cover the dough ball with a damp cloth and let rise at room temperature for about 2 hours, or until doubled in volume.

4. Divide the dough into two equal parts. Roll them both out on a floured work surface, forming two disks about 12 inches (30 cm) in diameter. Make a hole in the center of each and spread it out with your fingers, making a hole about 4 inches (10 cm) in diameter.

5. Lift the ends of each disk and bring them together, making them fit together to form an uneven ring-shaped loaf.

6. Arrange the loaves on a baking sheet lined with parchment paper. Cover them with a damp tea towel and let them rise again for 8 to 10 hours.

7. Preheat the oven to 400°F (200°C). Brush the surface of the dough with oil, if desired, and bake for 25 to 30 minutes, or until golden brown.

8. Remove from the oven and let cool completely on a wire rack.

Did you know...

Strazzata is a typical bread from Basilicata, and its special feature lies in its processing, which involves the tearing of the dough, that is, squashing and stretching it to give it its characteristic ring shape.

BASILICATA

PZETTO CHIENO

SAVORY EASTER PIE

Makes one 9-inch (23 cm) pie

INGREDIENTS

For the dough

300 g stone-ground whole wheat flour, plus more for dusting

700 g all-purpose flour

600 g water

4 g fresh brewer's yeast

10 g extra virgin olive oil

5 g salt

For the filling

200 g linguica sausage, chopped

100 g grated pecorino-Romano cheese

200 g provolone del monaco or provolone cheese

4 large eggs

5 g freshly ground pepper

RISE TIME

First rise: 1 hour

Proofing: 2 hours

BAKE TIME

30 minutes at 400°F (200°C)

1. Make the dough: In a large bowl, mix the two flours with the water and the brewer's yeast until smooth and evenly distributed. Add the oil and salt and work until combined.

2. Once the dough is smooth, let it rise for 1 hour at room temperature. Turn out the dough onto a floured pastry board or work surface, then divide it into two balls of the same size. Roll each into a 9-inch (23 cm) round.

3. Fill the pie: Grease a 9-inch (23 cm) baking pan and line it with one of the dough rounds. Arrange the chopped sausage, pecorino-Romano cheese, and provolone on top, and add the whole eggs inside the filling without breaking the yolks, and sprinkle with the pepper.

4. Cover the filling with the other disk of dough and seal the edges well. Let rise for a 2 hours at room temperature.

5. Preheat the oven to 400°F (200°C) and bake for about 30 minutes, or until the crust is golden brown.

Did you know...

This rich Lucanian savory pie—*chieno* means "stuffed" or "filled"—is linked to the Easter season, as easily guessed by the inclusion of eggs within the filling, which harden when baked.

SPORCAMUSS
PUFF PASTRY WITH CUSTARD

Makes about 30 small square pastries

INGREDIENTS

For the butter loaf
25 g all-purpose wheat flour
375 g butter, softened

For the puff pastry
10 g salt
50 g water
25 g butter, softened
250 g pastry or cake flour, plus more for dusting
250 g white spelt flour
2 eggs
85 g heavy cream
65 g white wine

For the pastry cream
500 g whole milk
Seeds from 1 vanilla bean
150 g egg yolks
150 g sugar
20 g cornstarch
20 g rice starch

For finishing
Confectioners' sugar

RISE TIME

Butter loaf: Overnight in the refrigerator
First rise: 30 minutes
Second rise: 30 minutes
Third rise: 30 minutes
Fourth rise: 30 minutes
Fifth rise: 30 minutes

BAKE TIME

18 to 20 minutes at 400°F (200°C)

1. Make the butter loaf: Combine the wheat flour and butter in a bowl and mix thoroughly. Lay parchment paper on a clean work surface, place the butter mixture on it, and cover with more paper. With a rolling pin, roll out the butter mixture until it forms a rectangle that is ¼ inch (6 mm) thick. Wrap the parchment around the butter and refrigerate overnight.

2. Make the puff pastry: In a large bowl, dissolve the salt in the water. Add the butter, both flours, eggs, cream, and wine, mixing until smooth. Wrap the dough in plastic wrap and let it rest in the refrigerator for 30 minutes, then roll it out on a lightly floured work surface and encase the butter loaf.

3. Fold the dough into four and place it back in the refrigerator for 30 minutes, then make a three-fold, like a letter, and place it back in the refrigerator for 30 minutes. Repeat the two operations and the resting times. In total, you will need to do four folds.

4. Make the pastry cream: Bring the milk to a boil in a medium saucepan with the seeds from a vanilla pod. In a small bowl, whisk the egg yolks with the sugar and starches. When the milk comes to a boil, temper the egg yolks by vigorously whisking in a small amount of milk. In batches, vigorously whisk in the remaining milk until the cream thickens. Pour it into a bowl and cover loosely with plastic wrap.

5. Roll out the puff pastry to a thickness of ⅙ inch (4 mm) and cut out 2-inch (5 cm) squares. Line a baking sheet with parchment paper. Preheat the oven to 400°F (200°C). Place the pastry on the prepared baking sheet and bake for 18 to 20 minutes, or until golden brown.

6. Once the puff pastries are out of the oven, let them cool, cut them in half, fill them with the cream, and close them like a sandwich, finishing with confectioners' sugar.

Did you know...

These are fragrant puff pastry sweets, typical of the city of Matera (but also widespread in Puglia, especially in the province of Bari). They are so called because it is almost impossible to eat them without smearing your face—*sporcamuss* is a local dialect term literally meaning to "get your face dirty"!

PITTA CALABRESE
CALABRESE RING BREAD

Makes 8 to 10 bread rings

INGREDIENTS

1 kg all-purpose flour, plus more for dusting

7 g fresh brewer's yeast

600 g water

22 g salt

60 g extra virgin olive oil

RISE TIME

First rise: Overnight in the refrigerator

Proofing: 4 hours

BAKE TIME

40 minutes at 450°F (230°C)

1. In a large bowl, mix the flour with the yeast and water until fairly smooth, then add the salt and oil and mix vigorously. When you have a smooth dough, put it in a large container, cover it with plastic wrap, and transfer it to the refrigerator. Let rise for 12 hours (overnight).

2. The next day, take the dough out of the refrigerator and turn it out onto a lightly floured pastry board or counter. Portion the dough and form into ring-shaped breads, then place them on a baking sheet lined with parchment paper and let rise for another 4 hours at room temperature.

3. Preheat the oven to 450°F (230°C) and bake the breads for about 40 minutes, until lightly golden.

Did you know...

Pitta is a thin, soft, ring-shaped bread popular throughout the region. It is excellent stuffed with *morzeddu* (offal), vegetables, or other Calabrian delicacies. The name is thought to derive from the Latin *picta*, meaning "decorated," referring to the fact that in Roman tradition it was originally a ritual food.

PIZZA RUSTICA
RUSTIC PIZZA

Makes 2 pizzas

INGREDIENTS

500 g all-purpose flour
500 g white whole wheat flour
670 g water
10 g fresh brewer's yeast
60 g extra virgin olive oil
22 g salt
300 g mild provolone cheese, diced
300 g *spianata* spicy salami

RISE TIME

First rise: 1 hour
Second rise: 30 minutes
Proofing: 2 hours

BAKE TIME

20 minutes at 475°F (240°C)

1. In a large bowl, mix the two flours with 600 g of the water and the brewer's yeast until smooth, then add the oil, salt, and remaining 70 g of water and work the mixture vigorously to make a smooth dough.

2. Top the dough: Add the diced provolone and *spianata* and stir to mix the ingredients well, then let rise for 1 hour at room temperature.

3. Divide the dough into 1-pound (500 g) balls. Transfer them to well-greased baking sheets and let rise for 30 minutes. Roll them out with your fingertips and let them rise for 2 more hours at room temperature.

4. Preheat the oven to 475°F (240°C) and bake for about 20 minutes, or until golden brown.

Did you know...

This tasty rustic pizza, perfect for a picnic, is a true essence of Calabrian flavors. In fact, the dough is enriched by two typical products of the region, and the sweetness of the cheese balances the spiciness of the sausage.

PITTA 'MPIGLIATA
CALABRIAN FRUIT AND NUT PASTRY

Makes 12 to 16 pastries

INGREDIENTS

For the dough

1 kg pastry or cake flour
16 g baking powder
500 g lard, at room temperature
250 g granulated sugar
4 large eggs
Pinch of salt
Grated zest of 1 lemon

For the filling

500 g dried figs, chopped
500 g raisins, soaked in water until plump
500 g walnuts, chopped
500 g almonds, chopped
100 g honey
50 g unsweetened cocoa powder
50 g anise liqueur
Grated zest of 1 orange
Pinch of ground cinnamon
Pinch of ground clove

For the garnish

Confectioners' sugar
Honey

RISE TIME

First rise: 1 hour

BAKE TIME

1 hour at 350°F (180°C)

1. Make the dough: Place the flour and baking powder in a large bowl, cut in the lard, and work the mixture with your hands until you have a sandy mixture.

2. Add the granulated sugar, eggs, salt, and grated lemon zest and mix until you have a smooth, homogeneous dough, then wrap it in plastic wrap and let it rise in the refrigerator for at least 1 hour.

3. Meanwhile, make the filling: Combine the chopped dried figs, drained raisins, chopped walnuts and almonds, honey, cocoa, liqueur, grated orange zest, cinnamon, and ground cloves in a large bowl and mix all the ingredients well.

4. Butter and flour a 9-inch (23 cm) round baking pan. Divide the dough into 2 portions. On a floured work surface, roll out one portion of dough to ⅛ inch (3 mm) thick. Line the prepared pan with the dough. Roll out the rest of the dough and, with a serrated pastry wheel, cut strips about 4 inches (10 cm) wide and at least twice as long. Place a little filling on each strip and roll the dough over itself lengthwise, shaping them into rosettes. Arrange the rosettes on the base pastry, trying to keep them close together.

5. Preheat the oven to 350°F (180°C). Bake for about 1 hour, or until the surface is golden brown.

6. Remove from the oven and let cool before garnishing the surface with confectioners' sugar and honey.

Did you know...

Pitta 'mpigliata or *'nchiusa* is an ancient dessert, originally from Sila, and is linked to the Christmas holidays, although it can now be eaten year-round. Its preparation requires some dexterity. The thin sheets, richly filled with dried fruit, are in fact formed into various shapes (the most common is the rosette), placed on top of the base, and enclosed (*'mpigliate*) by folding a small bit of dough.

MAFALDA
SICILIAN SESAME BREAD

Makes 2 loaves

INGREDIENTS

1 kg durum wheat semolina
680 g water
200 g solid sourdough starter (see page 76) (or 5 g fresh brewer's yeast)
22 g salt
Sesame seeds

RISE TIME

First rise: 1 hour
Second rise: 3 hours total (including 1 hour in the refrigerator)
Proofing: 2 hours

BAKE TIME

18 minutes at 475°F (240°C)

1. In a large bowl, mix the flour with 600 g of the water and let rise for about 1 hour at room temperature.

2. Add the sourdough starter and 60 g of water and continue mixing for 5 minutes. Then, add the salt and the remaining 20 g of water and continue mixing until smooth and homogeneous. Form into a ball and let it rise, covered, at room temperature for 2 hours. Transfer to the refrigerator to rise for 1 hour.

3. Divide the dough into two pieces, shaping each into a 24-inch (61 cm) long strand. Form a kind of serpentine with each one and pull the last several inches back along the middle of the serpentine (see photo).

4. Brush the surface with a little water and dredge it in sesame seeds. Place the loaves on a baking sheet lined with parchment paper and let the loaves rise one last time at room temperature for 2 hours.

5. Preheat the oven to 475°F (240°C) and bake for 18 minutes, or until golden brown.

Did you know...

The *Mafalda* is a Sicilian bread made from durum wheat semolina, characterized by its distinctive serpentine shape folded in on itself and covered with sesame seeds. It was apparently first made by a Catanian baker as a tribute to the then newly born Princess Mafalda of Savoy.

RIANATA

TRAPANI-STYLE PIZZA WITH OREGANO

Makes 3 medium pizzas

INGREDIENTS

For the dough

500 g all-purpose flour
500 g durum wheat semolina
700 g water
7 g brewer's yeast
22 g salt
50 g extra virgin olive oil

For the topping

Extra virgin olive oil, for brushing
10 anchovy fillets from a can, drained
3 garlic cloves, sliced
400 g peeled tomatoes
50 g grated pecorino-Romano cheese
1 bunch fresh oregano
Dried oregano, for topping

RISE TIME

First rise: Overnight in the refrigerator
Second rise: 2 hours at room temperature
Third rise: 30 minutes

BAKE TIME

25 minutes at 475°F (240°C)

1. Make the dough: In a large bowl, combine the flours with 600 g of the water and mix for 10 minutes. Add the brewer's yeast and another 50 g of water and continue to work the mixture vigorously. After 10 minutes, incorporate the salt and remaining 50 g of water, then slowly add the oil and knead the dough to absorb it well. Cover the bowl with plastic wrap, transfer to the refrigerator, and let rise overnight.

2. Divide the dough into three balls. Carefully place them on well-greased 9- or 10-inch (23 or 26 cm) round baking sheets and let rise for about 2 hours at room temperature.

3. Roll out the dough on the baking sheet a few times until it reaches the edges.

4. Brush the dough with extra virgin olive oil and add the topping: Arrange the anchovies and sliced garlic on the surface of the dough. Spread the tomatoes evenly and sprinkle with grated pecorino-Romano cheese. Let rise for 30 minutes.

5. Preheat the oven to 475°F (240°C). Bake for 25 minutes. Once the *rianata* is out of the oven, top with a pinch of dried oregano and plenty of fresh oregano.

Did you know...

Widespread throughout the province of Trapani and, especially, in the Ericino area, *rianata* is a pizza topped with lots of oregano, the ingredient that most distinguishes it by giving it a unique flavor and aroma. In the local dialect, the name actually means *origanata* ("flavored with oregano"). This Sicilian specialty is a De.Co (i.e., a municipal designation) product and therefore also has specifications for production.

CANNOLI

Makes 12 to 16 cannoli

INGREDIENTS

For the dough

1 kg all-purpose flour, plus more for dusting
120 g granulated sugar
5 eggs
6 g fine salt
120 g lard
40 g white wine vinegar
200 g Marsala wine
Grated zest of 1 orange
4 g ground cinnamon
Oil, for frying

For the filling

300 g sheep's-milk ricotta or whole-milk ricotta, drained
100 g confectioners' sugar, plus more for sprinkling
100 g chocolate chips
Candied orange peels

RISE TIME

First rise: 2 hours

BAKE TIME

Deep fried at 350°F (180°C) until golden brown

1. Make the dough: In a large bowl, combine the flour, granulated sugar, eggs, salt, lard, vinegar, wine, orange zest, and cinnamon. Mix until you obtain a smooth, homogeneous dough. Cover with plastic wrap and let rise for 2 hours in the refrigerator.

2. Roll out the dough on a floured work surface with a floured rolling pin to a thickness of ⅒ inch (2.5 mm). With a round 6-inch (15 cm) cookie cutter, cut out as many rounds as you can. Wrap them around a metal cannoli tube, pressing the ends together well.

3. Attach a deep-fry thermometer to a heavy, deep skillet. Pour in oil to a depth of 2 inches (5 cm) and heat the oil to 350°F (180°C). Add the cannoli shells and fry for 1 minute on each side, or until golden brown, then drain on paper towels and let cool.

4. Meanwhile, make the filling: In a large bowl, mix the ricotta cheese with the confectioners' sugar until creamy and smooth. Stir in the chocolate chips. Set aside.

5. Fill the cooled cannoli shells with the ricotta cream and garnish with candied orange peel (if you prefer, you can use chopped pistachios). Sprinkle with confectioners' sugar and serve. Remember to stuff the cannoli just before serving, otherwise the wafers will lose their crispness.

Did you know...

Of ancient Sicilian-Arab origin, cannoli are now among the most popular pastry delights throughout the peninsula. Stories and legends are told about its birth. According to one of the best known, the first to prepare it were the concubines of the harem that was based in Caltanissetta (the city's name comes from the Arabic *Qalat an-nisā* and means "women's castle"). Because of their large size, the cannoli from Piana degli Albanesi (Palermo) are renowned.

CIVRAXU

TRADITIONAL SARDINIAN SOURDOUGH BREAD

Makes 2 loaves

INGREDIENTS

1 kg twice-milled durum wheat semolina, plus more for dusting

800 g water

300 g solid sourdough starter (see page 76)

17 g salt

RISE TIME

First rise: 30 minutes

Second rise: 3 hours

Proofing: 3 hours

BAKE TIME

35 minutes at 450°F (230°C)

1. Combine the semolina and 750 g of the water in a bowl and mix with a spoon. The mixture should be coarse. Let it rise for at least 30 minutes at room temperature.

2. Add the sourdough starter and stir with the spoon, adding 25 g of water. Add the salt and remaining 25 g of water and mix for a few minutes, then cover the bowl with plastic wrap and let it rise for 3 hours at room temperature. After the first 40 minutes, fold the dough a few times, keeping it inside the bowl.

3. Divide the dough into two portions. Fold each portion on itself, keeping the closure at the bottom and giving them a round shape, then lay them on a tea towel sprinkled with semolina and let rise for 3 hours at room temperature.

4. Preheat the oven to 450°F (230°C) and line a baking sheet with parchment paper. Flip the loaves onto the prepared baking sheet and bake for about 35 minutes, until golden brown.

Did you know...

Also called *chivalzu*, *crivatzu*, or *civraxiu* depending on the area, this bread is prepared all over Sardinia, with particular prominence in Campidano and Sassarese. The versions from Sanluri (South Sardinia) and Osilo (Sassari) are very popular. The ground flour is usually made from durum wheat flour alone, from a mixture of durum wheat semolina and flour, or, especially in ancient times, from bran (the waste from flour refining); in the latter case, it is also called *pani nieddu* (black bread).

PIZZETTE DI SFOGLIA

SARDINIAN PUFF PASTRY PIZZETTAS

Makes 30 to 36 appetizer-size pizzas

INGREDIENTS

For the puff pastry

500 g butter
20 g sugar
26 g salt
500 g water
1 kg pastry or cake flour, sifted, plus more for dusting

For the topping

Tomato puree
Mozzarella, cut into cubes
Extra virgin olive oil
Basil pesto

RISE TIME

First rise: 2 hours in the refrigerator
Proofing: 30 minutes in the refrigerator

BAKE TIME

18 to 20 minutes at 425°F (220°C)

1. Make the puff pastry: Flatten the butter between two sheets of parchment paper. Wrap in plastic wrap and place in the refrigerator until ready to use.

2. In a large bowl, dissolve the sugar and salt in the water, then add the flour and mix until smooth. Let rise in the refrigerator for 2 hours.

3. Turn the dough out onto a floured pastry board, roll it out well, and encase the butter in the center. Close by pinching the edges together, then roll out the dough with a rolling pin to a thickness of ⅓ inch (8 mm) and fold in four. Cover with plastic wrap and transfer to the refrigerator for 30 minutes.

4. Preheat the oven to 425°F (220°C) and line a baking sheet with parchment paper.

5. Roll the dough to a thickness of about ⅙ inch (4 mm) and cut out small rounds 2 to 3 inches (2.5 to 8 cm) in diameter with a pastry cutter. Place the rounds onto the prepared baking sheet.

6. Top the pizzettas: Place a spoonful of tomato puree and a cube of mozzarella in the center of each round.

7. Bake for 18 to 20 minutes, or until golden brown, then remove the pizzettas from the oven and top with a drizzle of extra virgin olive oil and dollop of basil pesto.

Did you know...

Pizzette di sfogliate are delicious rustic puff pastries typical of Cagliari (in fact, they are also called *pizzette di cagliaritane*). They are never in short supply in the city's bars and pastry shops and are enjoyed at any time of the day, starting with breakfast and ending with an aperitif. The most traditional version involves two overlapping rounds of dough stuffed with tomato, mozzarella, oregano, and oil and brushed with beaten egg yolk before baking.

PARDULAS

RICOTTA AND SAFFRON TARTLETS

Makes about 16 tartlets

INGREDIENTS

For the dough

500 g twice-milled durum wheat semolina, plus more for dusting

250 g water

Pinch of salt

75 g lard

For the filling

500 g whole-milk ricotta cheese

250 g sugar

60 g egg yolks (from about 4 large eggs)

3 saffron threads

Grated zest of 1 lemon

Pinch of ground cinnamon

For brushing and topping

1 large egg, beaten

Sugar

RISE TIME

First rise: 30 minutes in the refrigerator

BAKE TIME

20 minutes at 350°F (180°C)

1. Make the dough: In a large bowl, combine the semolina with the water and salt and mix well. Cut in the lard and mix until a smooth, homogeneous dough forms. Wrap the dough in plastic wrap and let rise in the refrigerator for at least 30 minutes.

2. Meanwhile, make the filling: Use a fine-mesh sieve to drain excess liquid from the ricotta. Add it to a large bowl and mix in the sugar, egg yolks, saffron, lemon zest, and cinnamon. Mix until creamy, 1 to 2 minutes.

3. Dust a clean work surface with flour. Unwrap the dough and roll it out until 1/10 inch (3 mm) thick. Use a 3-inch (8 cm) round biscuit or pastry cutter to cut out rounds.

4. Place a spoonful of filling in the center of each round and use your fingers to pinch the corners of the pastry around the filling to give it the shape of a basket.

5. Preheat the oven to 350°F (180°C) and line a baking sheet with parchment paper.

6. Arrange the *pardulas* on the prepared baking sheet, brush the surface with beaten egg, and top with a pinch of sugar.

7. Bake for about 20 minutes, or until the *pardulas* are golden brown. Let cool completely before serving.

Did you know...

Pardulas are Sardinian sweets made with ricotta and saffron, traditionally prepared for the Easter holidays, now widespread and eaten throughout the island at all times of the year. Their shape resembles that of small baskets or radiant suns, given the characteristic points along the circumference, and the rich and creamy filling makes them truly irresistible. There are several versions: The most classic ones involve a pastry shell made from durum wheat semolina, as in this recipe.

CHAPTER 7

A PERFECT PANETTONE

Makes 4 panettones

INGREDIENTS

For the first yeast refreshment

50 g solid sourdough starter (see page 76)

50 g all-purpose flour

25 g water

For the second yeast refreshment

125 g solid sourdough starter (see page 76)

125 g all-purpose flour

60 g water

For the third yeast refreshment

200 g solid sourdough starter (see page 76)

200 g all-purpose flour

120 g water

For the first dough

230 g sugar

360 g water

800 g all-purpose flour

190 g solid sourdough previously refreshed

6 large egg yolks

230 g butter, softened

For the second dough

600 g raisins

230 g all-purpose flour

4 g diastatic malt powder (see Note)

230 g sugar

11 g salt

16 large egg yolks

30 g cocoa butter, melted

230 g butter

20 g honey

20 g orange paste

2 g grated orange zest

2 g grated lemon zest

Seeds scraped from 2 vanilla bean pods

290 g candied orange peel

120 g candied diamond citron or candied lemon peels

85 g unsalted butter

Make the first yeast refreshment: Around 7:00 in the morning, mix the starter, flour, and water in a container and let it triple in volume at a temperature of about 82°F (28°C) (if you can't find a place that is exactly 82°F [28°C], then look for a warm place in your house).

Make the second yeast refreshment: After 3½ hours, around 10:30 a.m., take 125 g of the previously refreshed sourdough starter and add, while stirring, the ingredients for the second refreshment. Let it rest again at 82°F (28°C) or in a warm place for 3½ more hours.

Make the third yeast refreshment: Around 2 p.m., or 3½ hours later, proceed with the third refreshment. Combine the listed ingredients in a container, mix, and let stand at about 82°F (28°C) or in a warm place until the dough triples in volume. If your room is cooler than 82°F (28°C), this may take a little longer.

Make the first dough: After about 4 hours (it will be about 6 p.m. at this point if you started at 7 a.m.) process the first dough. Dissolve the sugar in the water and add the flour. Use a handheld or stand mixer set to low to mix together the ingredients. Once a shaggy dough forms, add the previously prepared sourdough starter. Keeping the mixer on, slowly add the egg yolks and finally the butter. Once combined, transfer to a container that can hold three times the volume of the dough and let it rest at 79°F (26°C) (or in a warm place) for 12 to 14 hours.

Make the second dough: Meanwhile, soak the raisins in warm water for 12 hours. If you have followed the described time schedule, both the dough and the raisins should be ready for the next step at the same time. Drain the raisins.

It should now be the morning after you first started rehydrating the sourdough starter.

Add the flour to the first dough and knead well so that the mixture is stringy (i.e., forming a gluten mesh that is elastic and strong). Add the malt powder, sugar, and salt and mix until smooth. Next, slowly add the egg yolks. Let the mixture bind well and add the melted cocoa butter, butter, and honey. The mixture should have a soft, smooth, and silky consistency. While stirring, slowly add the orange paste, orange zest, lemon zest, vanilla seeds, candied orange peel, candied diamond citron, and drained raisins.

Let the dough rest for 1 hour at 79°F to 82°F (26°C to 28°C) or in a warm place, then divide into the desired weight. Roll out each section of dough, transfer to a baking mold or ramekin, and let rise for 6 to 8 hours at 79°F to 82°F (26°C to 28°C) until they reach the rim of the mold. Make a crosscut over the top of each loaf and insert a bit of unsalted butter in the center.

Preheat the oven to 350°F (180°C). Bake the dough until the thickest part reads 200°F (93°C) on an instant-read thermometer, about 50 minutes. Remove from the oven and turn upside down on a work surface, removing from the mold.

Take 8 to 10 metal or wooden skewers and push them through the panettone horizontally to help the panettone maintain its shape as it cools. Let cool for 5 to 6 hours.

If you can resist it, wait at least a couple of days before serving.

Note: This malt is rich in amylase enzymes that are capable of breaking down starches into sugars.

ABOUT THE AUTHOR

Born in Canelli (Asti), Italy, in 1986, Fulvio Marino grew up in the midst of the flours of Mulino Marino, the family business for which he still works. He has been telling the world about bread on TV since 2020 on Antonella Clerici's *È sempre mezzogiorno* (Rai1), has participated in *Bake Off Italia* (Real Time) as a judge, and since last year has been hosting *Il forno delle meraviglie,* a competition among bakers to discover Italian culinary excellence, and *Nel forno di casa tua*, a cooking school for home baking. He is the author of books focused on the world of baking, and, in September 2023, he opened FuocoFarina, a bakery with a restaurant in Alba.

ACKNOWLEDGMENTS

Being with people whom you look up to helps you grow and allows you to see the world from a new perspective. A book is certainly a mirror of the person you are at any given moment, but it is, above all, the result of interactions with those who walk alongside you.

This fourth book of mine is the result of continuous experimentation with "hands in the dough" research (in the truest sense of the word!), of travels, and of people I have met, and it chronicles, page after page, my journey in the world of baking. My passion has always been to discover recipes around Italy (and the world) and share them with those who have the same interests as me, trying to explain them in a simple way, within everyone's reach.

My family's relationship with Slow Food has ancient roots, dating back even to before I was born. We share the values and ideals of the association and consider them the foundation of our work, first and foremost "good, clean, and fair," as we believe bread should be. Thanks to all of the Slow Food editors, to Chiara Cauda, Carlo Bogliotti, Roberto Burdese, Federica Cammarata, Roberto Fidale, Benedetta Senin, and Federica Vizioli. Special thanks to Carlin Petrini, a great role model and source of inspiration. Without him I probably would not have written this wonderful book.

To my family and Mulino Marino (which are more or less the same thing), for always being there and because you can't make bread without (good) flour!

Thanks to Nadia, Maurilio, and Marco, my partners and fellow travelers in FuocoFarina, where my thoughts and work come to life and where you can come visit me to taste my recipes.

Thanks to all the wonderful team at the bakery and restaurant. It is the best team you could wish for!

Thanks to Stefano Bongiovanni and Francesca Sezzella, who worked tirelessly by my side to make all the recipes in this book. Once again, you have my gratitude.

Thanks to Eunice, who put up with me and supported me in this adventure as well. Her photos always portray the essence of people and recipes.

To Giulia and Carlotta, as indispensable as water and flour, thank you for being there and making me experience my work with happiness.

To Antonella Clerici, to whom I will be forever grateful: Your precious advice and insights appear in each of my books. Thank you from the bottom of my heart.

INDEX